Data Fabric

An Intelligent Data Architecture for AI

Steven Astorino

Mark Simmonds

MC Press Online, LLC

Boise, ID 83703 USA

Data Fabric: An Intelligent Data Architecture for AI

Steven Astorino and Mark Simmonds

First Edition
First Printing—November 2022

The following terms are trademarks or registered trademarks of International Business Machines Corporation in the United States, other countries, or both: IBM, the IBM logo, ibm.com, Watson™, With Watson™, IBM Cloud Pak™. A current list of IBM trademarks is available on the Web at *http://www.ibm.com/legal/copytrade.shtml*.

Other company, product, or service names may be trademarks or service marks of others.

While every attempt has been made to ensure that the information in this book is accurate and complete, some typographical errors or technical inaccuracies may exist. IBM does not accept responsibility for any kind of loss resulting from the use of information contained in this book. The information contained in this book is subject to change without notice. The publisher, authors, and IBM do not guarantee the accuracy of the book and do not assume responsibility for information included in or omitted from it.

MC Press offers excellent discounts on this book when ordered in quantity for bulk purchases or special sales, which may include custom covers and content particular to your business, training goals, marketing focus, and branding interest.

MC Press Online, LLC
Corporate Offices: 3695 W. Quail Heights Court, Boise, ID 83703-3861 USA
Sales and Customer Service: (208) 629-7275 ext. 500; service@mcpressonline.com
Permissions and Bulk/Special Orders: mc_bookstore@mcpressonline.com
www.mcpressonline.com • www.mc-store.com

ISBN: 978-1-58347-904-9

Acknowledgments

A special thank you to our contributors and collaborators, who helped make this book possible:

IBM contributors:

- *Jay Limburn, for the many data fabric–related blogs*
- *Kipruto Yego, for the blog "Augmented data management: Data fabric versus data mesh"*
- *Databand team, for the blog "Data observability: Everything you need to know"*
- *Roger E. Sanders, for preparation of illustrations, peer review of this book, and editing skills*

External contributors:

- *MC Press Online, for their editorial reviews and publishing*

Contents

Foreword

Many organizations recognize the value and benefits Artificial Intelligence (AI) can bring if implemented correctly. A long-standing challenge that many organizations continue to face is preparing their data and assets and making sure those are accessible, manageable, governed, and are of the right quality so that they can be consumed by new AI applications, applications that infuse AI across the enterprise to help ensure smarter business outcomes. This process is outlined in our previous book, *Artificial Intelligence: Evolution and Revolution*.

Over the years, numerous paradigms and efforts attempted to address the complexities of managing sprawling and disparate data silos that all seem to have fallen short of their promises and expectations. In addition, organizations need to put their data and assets where it makes most business sense, whether that's on-premises or in a private or public cloud, without detriment to their business operations and for the benefit of all.

This book attempts to explain the concepts and values that a data fabric can deliver to technical communities, such as developers, data scientists, and C-level IT executives, as well as business communities, such as business managers requiring self-service analytics and C-level business executives. A data fabric is a data management architecture that helps these technical communities optimize access to distributed data and intelligently curate and orchestrate it for self-service delivery to data consumers.

As we explain this from the viewpoint of our combined industry experience of more than 60 years, we hope you gain value and knowledge from our thoughts and insights.

While this book refers to some IBM products and approaches, it is not intended to endorse any product or company, although it draws from our own experiences of products that we have been exposed to during our journeys. The opinions expressed herein are our own and not those of any company for which either of us has worked.

Finally, we would like to thank our friends, our contributors, and most of all our families for their patience while we wrote this book. We hope you enjoy reading it as much as we enjoyed writing it.

Our best,

Steven Astorino and Mark Simmonds

> *"No matter how busy you may think you are, you must find time for reading, or surrender yourself to self-chosen ignorance."*
>
> *Confucius: 551 BC – 479 BC*

1

In the Beginning...

Data surrounds us. Every cell of every life form holds data of some sort. From the moment we are born, our senses send signals (data) to our brain that we continually process, creating yet more data as part of our thought processes. It's a never-ending cycle. To provide a context, it may be helpful to briefly explore how modern data processing evolved.

Since the very beginning of earliest civilizations, humankind has sought to share its thoughts and experiences with others through symbols such as drawings on cave walls, hieroglyphs in ancient tombs, ancient scrolls, papers, and books. As a species, our passion to learn and progress led to the desire and need to capture all this data, to store and share it for posterity and to pass our collective knowledge on to others as a means of building a civilization. The establishment of education delivered through scholastic programs and institutions helped formalize what we learn and how we learn. Educational, government, medical, public, and other organizations established their own libraries (the earliest forms dating back to 2600 BC), holding vast quantities of information, accessible for reference or for lending to patrons. Catalogs of this data have helped provide an indexed virtual representation of what is available, how it is stored, and where to find it, as well as often providing expert assistance from librarians or library technicians.

Early Data Storage and Management

In recent decades, analog recordings of audio, photos, and videos presented new dimensions of capturing data. Punched cards for gathering and processing early census data using tabulating machines appeared.

Recorded music on 78 rpm platters and "wire recorders" became a mainstay of radio. Magnetic tape emerged from the laboratory.

Information storage in most people's minds at the end of the World War II era meant books, filing cabinets or, to those at the leading edge of data processing technology, paper punch cards. Reels of tape, tape cartridges, and programmable computers were the stuff of science fiction. But in 1952 IBM announced the IBM 726, its first magnetic-tape unit, as shown in Figure 1.1. It shipped with the IBM 701 Defense Calculator. This innovation was significant because it was the first IBM large-scale electronic computer manufactured in quantity and was:

- IBM's first commercially available scientific computer

- The first IBM machine in which programs were stored in an internal, addressable, electronic memory

- Developed and produced in record time (less than two years from "first pencil on paper" to installation)

- Key to IBM's transition from punched-card machines to electronic computers with tape storage

Figure 1.1: An IBM 700 Series

IBM 701 Electronic Data Processing System included the IBM 701 electronic analytical control unit, IBM 706 electrostatic storage unit, IBM 711 punched-card reader, IBM 716 printer, IBM 721 punched-card recorder, IBM 726 magnetic-tape reader/recorder, IBM 727 magnetic-tape unit, IBM 731 magnetic-drum reader/recorder, IBM 736 power frame #1, IBM 737 magnetic-core storage unit, IBM 740 cathode-ray-tube output recorder, IBM 741 power frame #2, IBM 746 power distribution unit, and IBM 753 magnetic-tape control unit.

What followed was the advent of digital disk storage, which enabled organizations to collect and process more data faster than ever. In 1968, IBM launched the world's first commercial database-management system, called Information Control System and Data Language/Interface (ICS/DL/I). In 1969, it was renamed as Information Management System (IMS).

IBM's Database 2 (then abbreviated as DB2) traces its roots back to the beginning of the 1970s when Edgar F. Codd, a researcher working for IBM, described the theory of relational databases and in June 1970 published the model for data manipulation.

In 1974, the IBM San Jose Research center developed a relational Database Management System (DBMS), called System R, to implement Codd's concepts. A key development of the System R project was Structured Query Language (SQL). To apply the relational model, Codd needed a relational-database language he named DSL/Alpha. When IBM released its first relational-database product, it wanted to have a commercial-quality sublanguage as well, so it overhauled SEQUEL, and renamed the revised language Structured Query Language, a data-management language for relational databases still in use today.

The name "DB2" was first given to the DBMS in 1983 when IBM released DB2 on its MVS mainframe platform. (Source: https://en.wikipedia.org/wiki/IBM_Db2)

IBM and many other vendors continue to invest in relational and other forms of databases as they are one of the key technologies in online transactional processing (OLTP). IBM Db2, as it is known today, is also used for transaction analytics processing.

Relational databases have become the core technology for data warehouses and Master Data Management (MDM) systems (MDM systems are described below). In parallel to relational databases, other forms of data stores appeared, such as object-oriented, NoSQL, key value, wide-column store, and graph databases, to name but a few.

From Centralized to Distributed

For many years, data storage and processing were centralized. People had to take their work to the computer or access it through "dumb" terminals. With the advent of more affordable computers, processing and data became decentralized, putting computing power in the hands of individuals. However, this led to the problem of data being replicated in an uncontrolled manner.

With data being created, stored, and processed across many personal devices, it became increasingly difficult to control the sprawl of versions of data sets and apply standards of quality, security, and other controls. It didn't take long for individual departments in various enterprises to start organizing and storing just the data they needed. However, this gradually resulted in the problem of creating many data silos that usually didn't communicate with each other across the organization.

Master Data Management (MDM) is the discipline by which business and information technology work together to ensure the uniformity, accuracy, stewardship, semantic consistency, and accountability of the enterprise's official shared master data assets. Combined with data warehousing, MDM helps provide a 360-degree view of an entity, such as a person or product. (The reference to 360-degree view implies users should be able to look at an entity from many different perspectives to form a more complete understanding of that entity.) In a sense, MDM's creation was an attempt to recentralize some of the key data that was being held in disparate silos so it could be used across the whole organization as a trusted source of data—a single version of the truth, if you will. However, it still left the problem that there were often prime copies and distributed secondary copies of the data that needed to be kept synchronized to provide a source of truly trusted data.

Databases, OLTP, OLAP, Warehouses, Master Data Management, Marts, Lakes, Lakehouses, Hadoop

Numerous solutions appeared for managing and integrating data to enable reporting, analysis, and discovery of insights as data volumes grew. All of them were data stores given names such as database, OLTP, OLAP, data warehouses, MDM systems, data marts, data lakes, data lakehouses, and Hadoop. These terms tend to be used somewhat interchangeably at times. While the terms are similar, important differences exist that are explained in Appendix A. Each provides certain capabilities and values to different groups of users, but none was a panacea for all data management challenges, as originally hoped for when each was created. However, technology follows a maturity curve or cycle and these technologies eventually found their own niches as they matured.

Many forms of data stores and data servers are being used across the enterprise today. More variations of these, and new paradigms, will evolve in the future. Technology is constantly advancing. The authors of this book perceive the data fabric approach as offering enough longevity and flexibility to be able to integrate an organization's data assets and enable them for AI.

2

The Impact of Hybrid Cloud

A simple way to think of cloud computing is as the on-demand availability of computer system resources, especially data storage (cloud storage) and computing power, without direct active management by the user. Large cloud systems often have functions distributed over multiple locations, each location being a data center. Cloud computing relies on sharing of resources to achieve coherence and typically uses a "pay-as-you-go" model, which can help reduce capital expenses and help avoid unexpected operating expenses.

As a whole, all the different data stores mentioned in the previous chapter, when running in the cloud, give organizations various ways of being able to place their data and applications wherever it makes the best business sense for those enterprises to do so. Notwithstanding, some organizations may of course still face challenges running and managing cloud-based services. However, if done correctly, any organization can deliver major benefits to its cloud-service consumers.

The Goal of Cloud

The overall goal of cloud computing is to enable users to benefit from all data stores and cloud technologies without the need for deep knowledge or expertise in any of them. Cloud aims to cut costs and help the users focus on their core business without having to pay attention to how they access data beneath the covers.

The main enabling technology for cloud computing is virtualization. Virtualization software separates a physical computing device into one or more "virtual" devices, each of which can be used and managed individually to perform computing tasks. With operating system–level virtualization essentially creating a scalable system of multiple independent computing devices, enterprises can allocate and use their computing resources more efficiently. Virtualization provides the agility required to speed up IT operations and reduce costs by increasing infrastructure use. Autonomics helps automate the processes by which the organization can provision resources on demand. By minimizing user involvement, automation speeds up the course of action, reduces labor costs, and reduces the possibility of human errors.

Hybrid cloud, as shown in Figure 2.1, can have multiple configurations. It can be a composition of a public cloud and a private environment, such as a private cloud or on-premises resources, which remain distinct entities but are bound together, thus offering the benefits of multiple deployment models. Hybrid cloud can also mean the ability to connect colocated, managed, and dedicated services with cloud resources. Think of a hybrid cloud service as consisting of some combination of private, public, and community cloud services that are offered by different providers. A hybrid cloud service crosses isolation and provider boundaries that are sometimes needed to provide security and governance for multiple business entities or infrastructure providers. However, a hybrid cloud system can encompass many cloud styles and therefore cannot simply fit in a single category of private, public, or community cloud service. A hybrid structure enables an organization to extend either the capacity or the capability of a cloud service by aggregating, integrating, or customizing it with another cloud service. It's also important to understand that a hybrid cloud doesn't necessarily imply a private cloud is required for it to exist. The term simply means that different types of clouds can coexist with each other.

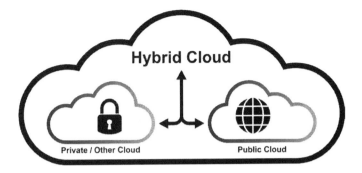

Figure 2.1: Hybrid cloud representation

Varied use cases for hybrid cloud composition exist. For example, an organization may store sensitive client data in-house on a private cloud application but interconnect that application to a business intelligence (BI) application provided on a public cloud as a software service. This example of hybrid cloud extends the capabilities of the enterprise to deliver a specific business service through the addition of externally available public cloud services.

Another example of a hybrid cloud is one where an IT organization uses public cloud computing resources to meet temporary capacity needs that cannot be met by a private cloud. This capability enables hybrid clouds to employ "cloud bursting" for scaling across clouds. Cloud bursting is an application-deployment model in which an application runs in a private cloud or data center and accesses additional resources ("bursts") from a public cloud only when the demand for computing capacity increases. A primary advantage of cloud bursting within a hybrid cloud model is that an organization pays for extra computing resources only when those resources are needed. Cloud bursting enables data centers to create an in-house IT infrastructure that supports average workloads but then use cloud resources from public or private clouds during spikes in processing demands.

A specialized model of hybrid cloud, which is built atop heterogeneous hardware, is called a "cross-platform hybrid cloud." A cross-platform hybrid cloud is usually powered by different CPU architectures–for example, x86-64 and Advanced RISC Machines (ARM) underneath. Users can transparently deploy and scale applications without knowledge of the cloud's hardware diversity. This kind of cloud emerges from the rise of ARM-based system-on-chip for server-class computing.

Hybrid cloud infrastructures essentially serve to eliminate limitations inherent to the multiaccess relay characteristics of private-cloud networking. The advantages include enhanced run-time flexibility and adaptive memory processing unique to virtualized interface models.

The Roles of Different "As a Service" Models

A key term in cloud computing is "as a service." This term implies that one or more elements of an infrastructure architecture (IA) can be presented as a consumable service while abstracting the complexities of the underlying technologies. The most important "as a service" models are as follows:

Infrastructure as a Service (IaaS) refers to online services that provide high-level APIs used to abstract various low-level details of underlying network infrastructures, such as physical computing resources, location, data partitioning, scaling, security, and backup services. Pools of hypervisors (software, firmware, or hardware that manages virtual machines) within the cloud operational system can support large numbers of virtual machines and can scale services up and down according to customers' varying requirements. Linux containers (self-contained processes) run in isolated partitions of a single Linux kernel (the core of an operating system), running directly on the physical hardware. Linux control groups (or "cgroups") and namespaces are the underlying Linux kernel technologies used to isolate, secure, and manage the containers. Containerization offers higher performance than virtualization because there's no hypervisor overhead. IaaS clouds often provide additional resources such as a virtual-machine disk-image library, raw block storage, file or object storage, firewalls, load balancers, IP addresses, virtual local area networks (VLANs), and software bundles.

The National Institute of Standards and Technology's (NIST) definition of cloud computing describes IaaS as "where the consumer is able to deploy and run arbitrary software, which can include operating systems and applications. The consumer does not manage or control the underlying cloud infrastructure but has control over operating systems, storage, and deployed applications; and possibly limited control of select networking components (e.g., host firewalls)."

IaaS cloud providers supply these resources on-demand from their large pools of equipment installed in data centers. For wide-area connectivity, customers can use either the Internet or carrier clouds (dedicated virtual private networks). To deploy their applications, cloud users install operating-system images and their application software on the cloud infrastructure. In this model, the cloud user patches and maintains the operating systems and the application software. Cloud providers typically bill IaaS services on a utility computing basis. The cost reflects the amount of resources the using entity allocates and consumes.

Platform as a Service (PaaS) is defined by NIST as "the capability provided to the consumer to deploy onto the cloud infrastructure consumer-created or acquired applications created using programming languages, libraries, services, and tools supported by the provider. The consumer does not manage or control the underlying cloud infrastructure including network, servers, operating systems, or storage, but has control over the deployed applications; and possibly configuration settings, for the application-hosting environment."

PaaS vendors offer a development environment to application developers. The provider typically develops toolkits and standards for development and channels for distribution and payment. In the PaaS models, cloud providers deliver a computing platform, typically an operating system, a programming-language execution environment, a database, and a web server. Application developers develop and run their software on a cloud platform instead of directly buying and managing the underlying hardware and software layers. With some PaaS, the underlying computer and storage resources scale automatically to match application demand so that the cloud user does not have to allocate resources manually.

Some integration and data management providers also use specialized applications of PaaS as delivery models for data. Examples include iPaaS (Integration Platform as a Service) and dPaaS (Data Platform as a Service). iPaaS enables customers to develop, execute, and govern integration flows. Under the iPaaS integration model, customers drive the development and deployment of integrations without installing or managing any hardware or middleware. Alternatively, dPaaS delivers integration (and data-management) products as fully managed services. Under the dPaaS model, the PaaS provider, rather than the customer, manages the development and execution of programs by building data applications for the customer. Users of dPaaS services access data through data-visualization tools.

Software as a Service (SaaS) as defined by NIST is "the capability provided to the consumer to use the provider's applications running on a cloud infrastructure. The applications are accessible from various client devices through either a thin client interface, such as a web browser (e.g., web-based email) or a program interface. The consumer does not manage or control the underlying cloud infrastructure including network, servers, operating systems, storage, or even individual application capabilities, with the possible exception of limited user-specific application configuration settings."

In the SaaS model, users gain access to application software and databases. Cloud providers manage the infrastructure and platforms that run the applications. SaaS is sometimes referred to as "on-demand software" and is usually priced on a pay-per-use basis or a subscription fee. Cloud providers install and operate application software via the cloud and cloud users access the software from cloud clients. Cloud users do not manage the cloud infrastructure and platform where the application runs. This eliminates the need to install and run the application on the cloud user's own computers, which simplifies maintenance and support. Cloud applications differ from other applications in their scalability, which can be achieved by cloning tasks onto multiple virtual machines at run time to meet changing work demand. Load balancers distribute the work over the set of virtual machines. This process is transparent to the cloud user, who sees only a single access point. To accommodate large numbers of cloud users, cloud-service providers can make applications multitenant, meaning that any machine may serve more than one cloud-user organization.

The pricing model for SaaS applications is typically a monthly or yearly flat fee per user, so prices become scalable and adjustable if users are added or removed at any point. It may also be free. Proponents claim that SaaS gives a business the potential to reduce IT operational costs by outsourcing hardware and software maintenance and support to the cloud provider. This enables the business to reallocate IT operations costs away from hardware/software spending and personnel expenses and instead toward meeting other goals. In addition, with applications hosted centrally, providers can release updates without requiring users to install new software.

Data as a Service (DaaS) is a term used to describe cloud-based software tools used for working with data, such as managing data in a data warehouse or analyzing data with BI applications. It is enabled by Software as a Service (SaaS). Like all "as a service" (aaS) technology, DaaS builds on the concept that its data product can be provided to the user on demand, regardless of geographic or organizational separation between provider and consumer.

As a business model, DaaS is a concept under which two or more organizations buy, sell, or trade machine-readable data in exchange for something of value. "Data as a service" can also be used as a general term that encompasses data-related services. DaaS service providers have been replacing traditional data analytics services or clustering with existing services to offer more value-addition to customers. The DaaS providers can curate, aggregate, and analyze multisource data to provide additional analytical data or information of value.

Typically, DaaS business is based on subscriptions and customers pay for a package of services or definite services. At the same time, investors must make sure that the revenue generated exceeds initial and operational costs of running the business. Because the customers only get access to the data stream delivered by DaaS vendors when they need it, DaaS eliminates the need to store data within a company and the corresponding costs, which makes the business more flexible. This can create a "shop for data" experience, a term related to DaaS that describes the ability of users inside an organization to collaborate on projects by creating, cataloging, consuming, and reusing data assets within or across multiple different projects.

Red Hat OpenShift Container Platform

The Red Hat OpenShift Container Platform is a platform for developing and running containerized applications. It is designed to enable applications and the data centers that support them to expand from just a few machines and applications to thousands of machines that serve millions of clients.

With its foundation in Kubernetes (an open-source container orchestration system), OpenShift Container Platform incorporates the same technology that serves as the engine for massive telecommunications, streaming video, gaming, banking, and other applications. Its implementation in open Red Hat technologies lets an organization extend their containerized applications beyond a single cloud to on-premises and multicloud environments. Although container images and the containers that run using them are the primary building blocks for modern application development, to run them at scale requires a reliable and flexible distribution system. Kubernetes automates deployment, scaling, and management of containerized applications and is widely considered the de facto standard for accomplishing these functions.

In only a few years, Kubernetes has seen significant cloud and on-premises adoption. The open-source development model lets developers extend Kubernetes by implementing different technologies for components such as networking, storage, and authentication.

Using containerized applications offers many advantages over using traditional deployment methods. Where applications were once expected to be installed on operating systems that included all their dependencies, containers let an application carry their dependencies with them.

Containers use small, dedicated Linux operating systems without a kernel. Their file system, networking, cgroups, process tables, and namespaces are separate from the host Linux system, but the containers can integrate with the hosts seamlessly when necessary. Being based on Linux enables containers to use all the advantages that come with the open-source development model.

Because each container uses a dedicated operating system, users can deploy applications that require conflicting software dependencies on the same host. Each container carries its own dependent software and manages its own interfaces, such as networking and file systems, so applications never need to compete for those assets. Because all the software dependencies for an application are resolved within the container itself, an organization can use a standardized operating system on each host in its data center. Users do not need to configure a specific operating system for each application host. When the data center needs more capacity, users can deploy another generic host system.

Similarly, scaling containerized applications is simple. The Red Hat OpenShift Container Platform as shown in Figure 2.2 offers a simple, standard way of scaling any containerized service. For example, if developers build applications as a set of microservices rather than large, monolithic applications, they can scale the individual microservices separately to meet demand. This capability lets an organization scale only the required services instead of the entire application, which can help the organization meet application demands with fewer resources.

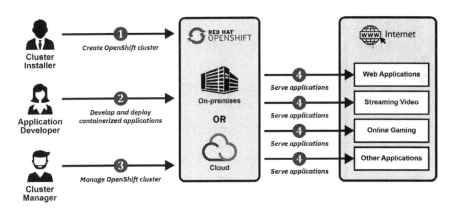

Figure 2.2: High-level OpenShift Container Platform overview

(Source: https://access.redhat.com/documentation/en-us/openshift_container_platform/4.8/
pdf/architecture/openshift_container_platform-4.8-architecture-en-us.pdf)

OpenShift Container Platform provides enterprise-ready enhancements to Kubernetes, including the following enhancements:

- Hybrid cloud deployments: Organizations can deploy OpenShift Container Platform clusters to a variety of public cloud platforms or in their data centers.

- Integrated Red Hat technology: Major components in OpenShift Container Platform come from Red Hat Enterprise Linux (RHEL) and related Red Hat technologies. OpenShift Container Platform benefits from the intense testing and certification initiatives for Red Hat's enterprise-quality software.

- Open-source development model: Development is completed in the open, and the source code is available from public software repositories. This open collaboration fosters rapid innovation and development.

Although Kubernetes excels at managing applications, it does not specify or manage platform-level requirements or deployment processes. Powerful and flexible platform management tools and processes are important benefits that OpenShift Container Platform 4.8 and later releases offer.

Many organizations will have multiple clouds, running across different hyperscalers (cloud services–based architectures that scale as increased demand is added to the system) as well as in on-premises environments. When implementing data and AI solutions, enterprises should always consider a vendor's capabilities to deliver and manage solutions in a hybrid multicloud environment that can offer the greatest flexibility to place organizational data, applications, and processes wherever it makes best business sense, recognizing that this may change over time as business needs evolve.

3

The Journey to AI

Cloud, containerization, Kubernetes, and Red Hat OpenShift together form one of the most portable platforms to host all of an organization's data and applications anywhere, regardless of whether it's on IBM Cloud or clouds of other providers. This is a great foundation. However, organizations often have hundreds of disparate apps and a growing number of data marts, databases, data warehouses, data lakes, and data lakehouses sprawled across and beyond the enterprise. Somehow these all need to be made seamlessly accessible to collect, organize, and analyze information and infuse AI into business processes and applications.

Some vendors or companies publish APIs that facilitate access to a range of data, Machine Learning (ML), and AI services. However, that alone still infers a level of technical ability that might be out of reach for many enterprises. APIs are just one small aspect of the overall data science experience. While some people may like to build a vehicle from a kit or individual components, most people prefer to buy a ready-to-drive vehicle that meets their long-term needs to take them on their many journeys.

The Best Performers Are Data-Driven

While many organizations are struggling with the challenges of data complexity, some organizations are finding success as they embrace a modern data strategy. Data-savvy organizations are more likely to leverage data in a manner that informs decision-making and to strategically address unmet needs with new data-driven business models. Only when an enterprise can provide organization-wide access to previously siloed data, configure governance policies, and address data-quality concerns is it ready to make large strategic AI investments that can ultimately lead to outperforming revenue targets and thereby increasing profitability.

The IBM Institute of Business Value (IBV) conducts regular surveys of organizations to identify market outperformers and looks for patterns that set them apart. The 20th edition of the C-suite study was published in 2020 and drew input from more than 13,000 respondents across multiple C-suite roles, industries, and countries. In the most recent edition of the study, companies were categorized based on their ability to create value from data and the degree to which they have integrated their data and business strategy. Identified as "torchbearers," 9 percent of companies surveyed have shown the most leadership in this area. There are some striking numbers in this study about these "torchbearer" companies:

- They are 88 percent more likely to make data-driven decisions to advance their corporate strategies.

- They are 112 percent more likely to find gaps and fill them with data-driven business models.

- They are 300 percent more likely to enable the free sharing of data across silos and different business functions.

- They are 149 percent more likely to make large strategic investments in AI technologies.

- Most importantly, they are 178 percent more likely to outperform others in their industry in the areas of revenue and profitability.

(Source: IBM Institute of Business Value Study of 13,000 C-suite leaders: https://www.ibm.com/thought-leadership/institute-business-value/c-suite-study)

The bottom line: The enterprise must outperform its competitors or risk being outperformed by them.

What IBM has learned from countless AI projects is that every step of the journey is critical. AI is not magic; it requires a thoughtful and well-architected approach. For example, most AI failures are due to problems in data preparation and data organization, not the AI models themselves.

Success with AI models depends on achieving success first with how the enterprise collects and organizes the data.

The AI Ladder, shown in Figure 3.1, represents a prescriptive approach to help customers overcome data challenges and accelerate their journey to AI, no matter where they are on their journey. It enables them to simplify and automate how an organization turns data into insights by unifying the collection, organization, and analysis of data, regardless of its location. By climbing the ladder to AI, enterprises can build a governed, efficient, agile, and future-proof approach to AI.

The AI Ladder has four steps (often referred to as "rungs"):

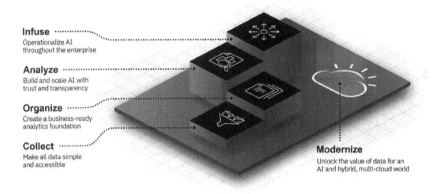

Figure 3.1: Four steps of the AI Ladder

1. *Collect: Make data simple and accessible.* Collect data of every type, regardless of where it lives, enabling flexibility in the face of ever-changing data sources. Note that "collect" does not mean put all the data in one place. In fact, quite the opposite. It means virtualizing the data, enabling access to it as if it were consolidated.

2. *Organize: Create a business-ready analytics foundation.* Organize collected data into a trusted, business-ready foundation with built-in governance, protection, and compliance.

3. *Analyze: Build and scale AI with trust and transparency.* Analyze data in automated ways and benefit from AI models that empower teams to gain new insights and make better, smarter decisions.

4. *Infuse: Operationalize AI throughout the business.* Infuse AI throughout the business (across multiple departments and within various processes), drawing on predictions, automation, and optimization.

These steps can be further broken down into a set of key capabilities, shown in Figure 3.2.

Figure 3.2: AI Ladder capabilities

Supporting the AI Ladder is the concept of modernization, which is how customers can simplify and automate the way they turn data into insights by unifying the collection, organization, and analysis of data within a secure hybrid cloud platform.

The following priorities are built into the IBM technologies that support this AI ladder:

- Simplicity: Different kinds of users can leverage tools that support their skill levels and goals, from "no code" to "low code" to programmatic.

- Integration: As users go from one rung of the ladder to the next, the transitions are seamless.

- Automation: The most common and important tasks have intelligence baked into them so that users focus on innovation rather than repetitive tasks.

4

Reducing Complexity with a Data Fabric

Enterprises face all sorts of complexities in implementing their data use cases using current approaches, such as providing a 360-degree view of the data and MDM use cases, regulatory compliance, operational analytics, BI, and data science, to name a few.

As many infrastructures grow, enterprises can often face higher compliance, security, and governance risks. This can result in complexity and a higher level of effort to enforce policies and perform stewardship. Complex infrastructures can lead to higher costs for integrating data and stitching data pipelines across multiple platforms and tools. In turn, these can bring more reliance on IT, making collaboration more challenging and possibly slowing time to value. Alternatively, business-led self-service analytics, insights, and democratization of data (the ongoing process of enabling authorized users to access and work with data more easily without relying solely on an IT staff for help) could help deliver greater business agility. There have been many attempts to pull disparate data silos together, but nearly all fell short of business and user expectations as data volumes and the variation of data types that had to be managed grew.

The advancements made with databases, warehouses, data lakes, and lake houses, along with evolution among the modern cloud hyperscalers, as well as solutions that enable data to be much more distributed and the increasingly critical need to gain insights from data to differentiate an enterprise from its competitors, have collectively been driving a cultural shift to the approach of how data is managed.

What's needed is a new design or approach that provides an abstraction layer to share and use data, that includes built in with data and AI governance, across a hybrid cloud landscape—without a massive pendulum swing back to having everything decentralized. It's a matter of striking a balance between what needs to be logically or physically decentralized and what needs to remain centralized. For example, an enterprise can have multiple data catalogs, but there can be only one source of truth for the organization's global data catalog. The answer is the concept of a data fabric.

A data fabric is a data management architecture that helps optimize access to distributed data and intelligently curate and orchestrate it for self-service delivery to data consumers. Some of a data fabric's key capabilities and benefits are:

- Architected to help elevate the value of enterprise data by providing users with access to the right data just in time, regardless of where or how it is stored

- Architecture-agnostic to data environments, data processes, data use, and geography, while integrating core data management capabilities

- Ability to automate data discovery, governance, and consumption, delivering business-ready data for analytics and AI

- Ability to help business users and data scientists access trusted data faster for their applications, analytics, AI and ML models, and business process automation so as to improve decision-making and drive digital transformation

- Ability to help technical teams use simplified data management and governance in complex hybrid and multicloud data landscapes while significantly reducing costs and risk

In essence, a data fabric is an architecture that facilitates the end-to-end integration of various data pipelines and cloud environments via intelligent and automated systems. Over the last decade, developments within hybrid cloud, artificial intelligence, the Internet of Things (IoT), and edge computing have led to the exponential growth of Big Data, creating even more complexity for enterprises to manage. This has made the unification and governance of data environments an increasing priority as this growth has fueled significant challenges, such as increased siloing of data, security risks, and general bottlenecks for decision-making. Data management teams are addressing these challenges head on with data fabric solutions. They are leveraging data fabric concepts to unify their disparate data systems, embed governance, strengthen security and privacy measures, and provide more data accessibility to workers, particularly their business users.

These data integration efforts enable more holistic, data-centric decision-making. Historically, an enterprise may have had different data platforms aligned to specific lines of business. For example, it might have an HR data platform, a supply-chain data platform, and a customer data platform, each of which houses data in different and separate environments despite potential overlaps. However, a data fabric can enable decision-makers to view this data more cohesively to better understand the customer lifecycle, making connections between data points that weren't discrete before. By closing these gaps in understanding of customers, products, and processes, data fabrics are accelerating digital transformation and automation initiatives across businesses.

The data fabric approach can help enable organizations to better manage, govern, and use data to balance agility, speed, service-level agreements, and trust. Trust includes deep enforcement of governance, security, and compliance policies. Enterprises must also take into account the total cost of ownership and performance (TCO/P). This includes integration costs, egress costs, bandwidth costs, and processing costs vs. performance, among other issues. A data fabric could offer these benefits by degrees that are orders of magnitude greater than existing solutions to meet the complexities often seen across many enterprise infrastructures.

Data Fabric vs. Data Mesh

To eliminate possible confusion, it's important to distinguish between a data fabric and a data mesh. While not the focus of this book, a data mesh architecture is an approach that aligns data sources by business domains, or functions, with data owners. With data ownership decentralization, data owners can create data products for their respective domains, meaning that data consumers (both data scientists and business users) can use a combination of these data products for data analytics and data science.

The value of the data mesh approach is that it helps shift the creation of data products to subject matter experts upstream who know the business domains best, as compared to relying on data engineers to cleanse and integrate data products downstream.

Furthermore, the data mesh accelerates reuse of data products by enabling a publish-and-subscribe model (in which messages about application building blocks are sent to affected subscribers) and leveraging APIs, which makes it easier for data consumers to get the data products they need, including reliable updates.

A data fabric and data mesh can co-exist. Below are three ways a data fabric enables the implementation of a data mesh:

1. Provides data owners with capabilities that offer data asset creation capabilities like cataloging data assets and transforming assets into reusable services, and that comply with federated governance policies

2. Enables data owners and data consumers to use the capabilities to publish data assets to the catalog, search and find data assets, and query or visualize data assets by leveraging data virtualization or using published APIs

3. Enables leveraging of insights from data fabric metadata to automate tasks by learning from patterns as part of the data asset creation process or as part of the process of monitoring data assets

Table 4.1 shows a comparison of a data fabric and a data mesh.

	Data Fabric	Data Mesh
What It Is	An architectural, focused approach reducing human involvement. It relies on automation to orchestrate data regardless of source. Self-service access to unified and governed data are key tenets.	An approach centered on an organizational process to enable agile, domain-specific ownership and creation of reusable data products. It is technology-agnostic, and domain owners are responsible for the entire data lifecycle.
Key Attributes	Data integration approach. Reduces human effort. Platform- and automation-based. Unified singe view of data based on underlying metadata. Data is a byproduct. Centralized governance is critical. Adherents are primarily platform and tool providers.	Data ownership approach. Shifts human effort to domains. Data is the product. Data remains distributed (accessed and combined as needed). Federated governance to enable data product interoperability standards. Adherents are service/technology implementers.
What Challenges It Addresses	Increasing data silos, volumes, and sources. Complex IT environments. Bottlenecks that result from centralized data architectures and skills.	Increasing data silos, volumes, and sources. Complex IT environments. Bottlenecks that result from centralized data architectures and skills.
Benefits	Automates data management to reduce human burden and costs, eliminates the data bottlenecks that impede scalability and agility, enables self-service analytics and a single view of data.	Eliminates the data bottlenecks that impede scalability and agility, enables an agile data-product culture that creates more business value, enables domain-based service analytics.
Considerations	Data Mesh advocates may assert that automation cannot deliver as promised and those with business context are not empowered. May be perceived as more complex than data-platform investments.	Requires significant organizational and cultural change. May remove bottlenecks but introduce other data management challenges, including governance. May require addition of resources
Market Interest	Higher volumes of stories, social media mentions, and, until recently, Google search volumes. Words such as "scalable," "governance," "trust," and "integration" are associated with Data Fabric.	Stories and Google search volumes have been trending upward. Words or phrases such as "data ownership" and "democratization" are associated with Data Mesh. Rising interest in Mesh due to increasing number of implementers.

Table 4.1: Data fabric and data mesh comparison

Delivering a Data Fabric as Part of a Hybrid Cloud Data and AI Platform

IBM delivers its data fabric capabilities as part of its data and AI platform, Cloud Pak for Data, as shown in Figure 4.1. It embodies everything mentioned above, usually offered in a unified Enterprise Insight Platform (EIP) that runs on multiple vendors' clouds and infrastructures. EIP is a term used by industry analysts and consultants as a category for describing such integrated sets of data management, analytics, and development tools.

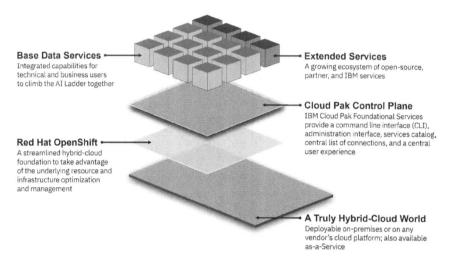

Base Data Services
Integrated capabilities for technical and business users to climb the AI Ladder together

Extended Services
A growing ecosystem of open-source, partner, and IBM services

Cloud Pak Control Plane
IBM Cloud Pak Foundational Services provide a command line interface (CLI), administration interface, services catalog, central list of connections, and a central user experience

Red Hat OpenShift
A streamlined hybrid-cloud foundation to take advantage of the underlying resource and infrastructure optimization and management

A Truly Hybrid-Cloud World
Deployable on-premises or on any vendor's cloud platform; also available as-a-Service

Figure 4.1: Cloud Pak for Data

The first core tenet of Cloud Pak for Data is that it can run anywhere. An enterprise can co-locate it anywhere the organization is making its infrastructure investments. This means enterprises can deploy Cloud Pak for Data on many major cloud vendor's platforms, as well as the IBM Cloud. It can also be deployed on-premises for hybrid cloud environments. Finally, on IBM Cloud, enterprises can subscribe to Cloud Pak for Data as a Service (DaaS) if they need a fully managed option where the consumer pays for only what it uses. Cloud Pak for Data gives organizations the deployment flexibility to run anywhere.

Cloud Pak for Data is built on the foundation of Red Hat OpenShift. This provides the flexibility that lets customers scale across any infrastructure using the leading open-source steward: Red Hat. Red Hat OpenShift is a Kubernetes-based platform that enables IBM to deploy software through a container-based model, delivering greater agility, control, and portability.

IBM's Cloud Pak offerings also share a common control plane, which makes administration and integration of diverse services easy.

Cloud Pak for Data includes preintegrated data services that let users collect information from any repository, such as databases, data lakes, and data warehouses. The design point here is to enable the enterprise to leave the data in all the places where it already resides but to make it seem to enterprise users that the enterprise data remains in one spot.

Once the enterprise connects all of its data, it can deploy data-organization services that facilitate developing an enterprise data catalog. This capability enables a "shop for data" type of experience and enforces governance rules across all data sources, thereby providing data consumers with a single point of access for their data needs.

With enterprise data connected and cataloged, Cloud Pak for Data presents a wide variety of data analysis tools right out of the box—for example, data science capabilities that cater to all skill levels (meaning no-code, low-code, and all code). Users can grab data from the catalog and instantly start working toward generating insights in a common workflow built around the "project" concept. For instance, users could create an analytics project to work with data and other assets to achieve a particular goal, such as building a model or integrating data.

Cloud Pak for Data includes extended services that provide an expanded set of capabilities, such as more specialized data management and analytics features. These range from powerful IBM solutions, like Planning Analytics with Watson, to solutions from IBM Partners that offer business ontology creation, open-source databases, and more.

Automation: The Key to Agility

Cloud Pak for Data takes automation to the next level. Watson Query capabilities let enterprises leave their data where it resides and connect to all structured or unstructured data sources in the enterprise without data movement. Building on that data collection, AutoCatalog and AutoPrivacy supercharge data discovery and ensure enforcement of governance policies across many sources and users. On top of this,

AutoAI makes it easy for data analysts and data scientists to generate new models in a fast, low-code manner with an award-winning graphical interface and design. Figure 4.2 summarizes these features.

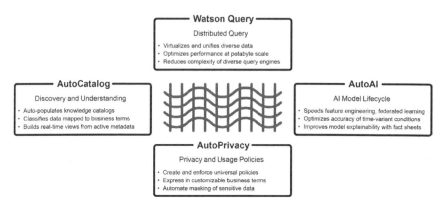

Figure 4.2: Automation capabilities within Cloud Pak for Data

Let's dive a little deeper into some of these automation capabilities.

- *Watson Query* is a high-performance, universal query engine that simplifies the data landscape by enabling clients to use the same query across disparate data sources, including data warehouses, data lakes, and streaming data, thereby saving time and resources that would typically go into moving data and maintaining multiple query engines. In conjunction with the platform's existing data virtualization capabilities, Watson Query empowers users to query data across hybrid, multicloud, and multivendor environments. Watson Query includes preintegrated data governance capabilities, so data consumers are assured of the quality and validity of the data.

- *AutoCatalog* automates how data is discovered and classified to maintain a real-time catalog of data assets and their relationships across disparate data landscapes. A critical capability of the intelligent data fabric within the platform, AutoCatalog helps overcome the challenges faced by managing a complex hybrid and multicloud enterprise data landscape and helps ensure that data consumers can find and access the right data, at the right time, regardless of location.

- *AutoPrivacy* employs AI to intelligently automate the identification, monitoring, and, subsequently, enforcement of policies on sensitive data across the organization. AutoPrivacy is a key aspect of the universal data privacy framework available within IBM Cloud Pak for Data. Spanning the entire data and AI lifecycle, this framework lets business leaders provide the self-service access data consumers need without sacrificing security or compliance. This helps enterprises build a better strategy for governance risk and compliance by eliminating compliance "blind spots" and minimizing risk.

- *AutoAI* automates data preparation, model development, and feature engineering to train and deploy top-performing models in minutes. It simplifies AI lifecycle management to build models faster and to accelerate deployment, and it opens AI to broader skill sets.

Data and AI: How and Where the Users Need It

IBM's open information architecture for AI is built on Cloud Pak for Data on Red Hat OpenShift for a hybrid cloud world. What does this mean? In one word, flexibility. To further explain, consider the following:

- If an organization is in a place where it needs to manage as little IT as possible, users can consume Cloud Pak for Data entirely through an as-a-service model by subscribing to the integrated family of data services on the IBM Cloud.

- If an organization needs the flexibility and control of running the data infrastructure in its own data center, or on IaaS from a preferred cloud vendor, it can deploy OpenShift and then Cloud Pak for Data on its local or cloud estate.

- If high performance and total control are needed, the enterprise can choose the Cloud Pak for Data System, which is a hyper-converged infrastructure (an optimized appliance) that combines compute, storage, and network services that are tailored for OpenShift and data and AI workloads.

Regardless of the form factor and the degree of management control needed, Cloud Pak for Data provides cloud-native data-management services that modernize how businesses collect, organize, and analyze data and then infuse AI throughout their organizations.

In summary, Cloud Pak for Data is designed to provide a unified, integrated user experience to collect, organize, and analyze data and infuse AI throughout the enterprise using the data fabric approach and architecture. Much of the complexities of managing and orchestrating data and other artifacts can be abstracted through the data fabric architectural approach. Think of the data fabric as the "magic" that can help make more of an organization's data, applications, and services ready for AI by automating and augmenting many of the steps that would otherwise have to be undertaken by large groups of architects, administrators, and data scientists.

5

The Data Fabric Advantage

The data fabric architecture that is provided by Cloud Pak for Data enables organizations to accelerate data analysis for better, faster insights.

The capabilities of the Cloud Pak for Data data fabric architecture are designed to help organizations:

- Simplify and automate access to data across multicloud and on-premises data sources, without moving data

- Universally safeguard the use of all data, regardless of source

- Provide business users with a self-service experience for finding and using data

- Use AI-powered capabilities to automate and orchestrate the data Lifecycle

Figure 5.1 shows the five main capabilities of the data fabric and the connectivity between the platform and existing data sources.

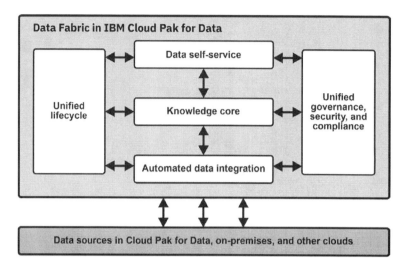

Figure 5.1: Five main capabilities of the data fabric as delivered by IBM Cloud Pak for Data

One duty of data stewards (who oversee an organization's data assets to ensure they are usable, accessible, trusted, and safe) is to enrich data with metadata that describes the data and makes it easier for users to find. They curate data into catalogs more expeditiously when assisted by automated discovery and classification of the data. They can further enrich data assets by creating and assigning custom governance artifacts, such as business vocabulary definitions. They can also import ready-to-use collections of metadata from industry-specific Knowledge Accelerators. (IBM components: Watson Knowledge Catalog service, Knowledge Accelerators)

Data scientists and other business users can find the data that they need in data catalogs that contain data from across the enterprise. They can browse for data, view their peers' highly rated assets, or use AI-powered semantic search and recommendations that consider asset metadata. This facilitates "a shop for data" experience and lets users add and copy data assets from a catalog into a project, where they can collaborate to prepare, analyze, and model the data.

Data stewards can also create data protection rules to automatically enforce uniform data privacy across the platform. Data masking identifies sensitive data to provide data security while it preserves data utility and prevents the need for multiple copies of the data. (IBM Components: Watson Knowledge Catalog service, Knowledge Accelerators)

Data integration can be a time-consuming and arduous task for IT departments. Using AI to automate the discovery, enhance the quality, and facilitate integration of the data can help accelerate the time-to-value and ROI of a project. A data fabric helps data engineers and other users prepare an organization's data for consumption. They can provide access to data within an existing data architecture and automate data preparation. They can integrate and virtualize data for faster, simpler querying. They can automate the bulk ingestion, cleansing, and complex transformations of data to regularly publish updated data assets. They can move the processing of the data to the data's location. (IBM components: Cloud Pak for Data platform, Data Refinery tool, Data Virtualization service, DataStage service)

Users can design, build, test, orchestrate, deploy to production, and monitor different types of data pipelines in a unified way. Users can create or find data assets, search for them across the platform, and move them across workspaces. Users can orchestrate data transformations and other actions by scheduling jobs that run automatically. (IBM components: Cloud Pak for Data platform)

Data Fabric vs. Data Virtualization

Data virtualization is the ability to view, access, and analyze data without the need to know its location. It can integrate data sources across multiple data types and locations, turning it into a single logical view without having the need to do any sort of data replication or movement. Data virtualization is also one of the technologies that enables a data fabric approach. Rather than physically moving the data from various on-premises and cloud sources using the standard Extract, Transform, Load (ETL) processes, a data virtualization tool connects to the different sources, integrating only the metadata required and creating a virtual data layer. This lets users leverage the source data in real-time, alleviating the need to move the data.

By leveraging data services and APIs, data fabrics pull together data from legacy systems, data lakes, data warehouses, SQL databases, and applications, providing a holistic view into business performance. In contrast to these individual data storage systems, a data fabric aims to create more fluidity across data environments, attempting to counteract the problem of data gravity (the idea that data becomes more difficult to move as it grows). A data fabric abstracts away the technological complexities engaged for data movement, transformation, and integration to make all data available across the enterprise.

Data fabric architectures operate around the idea of loosely coupling data in platforms with applications that need it. One example of a data fabric architecture in a multicloud environment is shown in Figure 5.2. It is common that one cloud, such as AWS or IBM Cloud, manages data ingestion, and another platform, such as Azure or IBM z Systems, oversees data transformation and consumption.

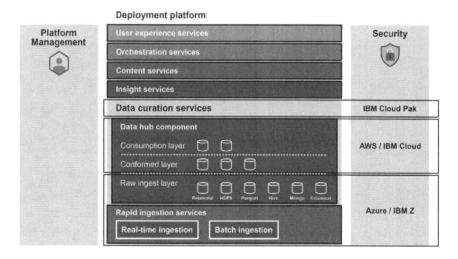

Figure 5.2: A data fabric architecture

Then there might be a situation in which there is a separate vendor with their Data and AI platform, like IBM with Cloud Pak for Data, providing analytical services. The data fabric architecture can stitch these environments together to create a unified view of data.

However, this is just one example. There isn't a single data architecture for a data fabric because different businesses have different needs. The various number of cloud providers and data infrastructure implementations ensure variation across businesses. Figure 5.3 shows an example of how data and other services across a hybrid multicloud environment can be leveraged more transparently using the data fabric design and approach. However, businesses using this type of data framework exhibit commonalities across their architectures, which are unique to a data fabric. More specifically, they have multiple fundamental components or layers:

1. Data management: This layer is responsible for data governance and security of data.

2. Data ingestion: This layer begins to stitch cloud data together, finding connections between structured and unstructured data.

3. Data processing: This layer refines the data to ensure that only relevant data is surfaced for data extraction.

4. Data orchestration: This critical layer conducts some of the most important jobs for the data fabric: transforming, integrating, and cleansing the data, making it usable for teams across the business.

5. Data discovery: This layer surfaces new opportunities to integrate disparate data sources. For example, it might find ways to connect data in a supply chain data mart and customer relationship management data system, enabling new opportunities for product offers to clients or ways to improve customer satisfaction.

6. Data access: This layer enables the consumption of data, ensuring the right permissions for certain teams to, for example, comply with government regulations. Additionally, this layer helps surface relevant data via dashboards and other data visualization tools.

Cloud Pak for Data and the Data Fabric in action

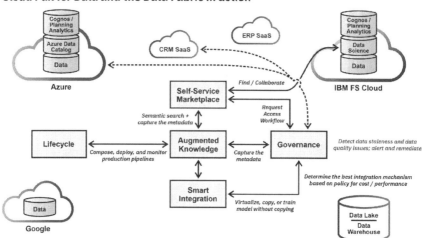

Figure 5.3: How data and other services across a hybrid multicloud environment can be leveraged more transparently using the data fabric design and approach

Other Advantages of Data Fabric Architectures

As data fabric providers gain more market share from businesses in the market, some analysts have noted specific improvements in efficiency, to the effect that a data fabric can reduce time for integration design by 30 percent, deployment by 30 percent, and maintenance by 70 percent. While it's clear that data fabrics can improve overall productivity, the following benefits have also demonstrated business value for adopters:

- Intelligent integration: Data fabrics use semantic knowledge graphs (a network of real-world entities such as objects, events, situations, or concepts, illustrating the relationship between them), metadata management, and ML to unify data across various data types and endpoints. This aids data management teams in clustering related data sets together as well as integrating new data sources into a business's data ecosystem. This functionality automates aspects of data workload management to create potential efficiency gains, as well as helps to eliminate silos across data systems, centralize data governance practices, and improve overall data quality.

- Democratization of data: Data fabric architectures facilitate self-service applications, broadening the access of data beyond more technical resources, such as data engineers, developers, and data analytics teams. Data democratization can help reduce data bottlenecks, subsequently fostering more productivity, enabling business users to make faster business decisions and freeing up technical users to prioritize tasks that better utilize their skillsets.

- Better data protection: The broadening of data access doesn't mean compromising on data security and privacy measures. In fact, it means that more data governance guardrails are put into place around access controls, ensuring that specific data is only available to certain roles. Data fabric architectures also let technical and security teams implement data masking and encryption around sensitive and proprietary data, mitigating risks associated with data sharing and system breaches.

6

Data Fabric, DataOps, and the Data Catalog

A data fabric can help connect, govern, and protect siloed data distributed across a hybrid cloud landscape and can help bring a data strategy to life. To reach that goal, enterprises need an end-to-end data science platform that provides user self-service access and integrated, supported, and automated tools for model building and continual delivery of models to production. Such a platform should:

- Unify data and AI capabilities together on an integrated platform

- Simplify data integration by automating engineering tasks

- Automate governance, data protection, and security enabled by active metadata

- Provide collaborative tools

- Provide purpose-built AI model risk management

As a solution, many organizations have begun to implement data operations (DataOps). DataOps orchestrates people, processes, and technology to solve the challenges associated with inefficiencies in accessing, preparing, and integrating data. This enables collaboration across an organization to drive agility, speed, and new initiatives at scale. It aims to deliver continuous enterprise data that is high-quality and trustworthy.

At the heart of an effective DataOps practice is a data catalog, a metadata management tool designed to help organizations find and manage large amounts of data. It puts trusted data in the hands of a business by automating the organization of a common and known business vocabulary, self-service management of data, and on-boarding of data content. From supporting multicloud adoption and integration, to accelerating an organization's journey to AI, the data catalog is foundational.

As the quantity of data available to organizations has grown exponentially over the last several years, data catalogs have grown in importance and their definition and scope have grown as well. Delivering business-ready data to feed analytics and AI projects begins with a data catalog that can automate organization, provide consistent definitions, and enable self-service management of enterprise data. A modern data catalog enables data analysts to find all the data available in each database or application maintained by their organization. This can include both relational data and unstructured data that can be found in MS Word documents or spreadsheets, as well as analytic assets that could include Jupyter Notebooks, trained models, and dashboards. Because data catalogs make data sources more discoverable and manageable, they help organizations make more informed decisions about how to use their data. The kind of information that should be embedded inside data assets includes how to access the data, the data format, the classification of the asset, the asset lineage, and the list of collaborators that have access to certain kinds of data.

Data Catalog Attributes and Benefits

When looking for a data catalog, it is essential for the catalog to have a metadata repository that acts as an index for data and other assets, making it easier for users to understand what kind of data and analytic assets are in the catalog. Here's how a data catalog can smoothly ensure the addition of assets:

- It leaves enterprise data where it is and lets users simply add the connection information to the date catalog to provide access, whether it is in the cloud or on-premises.

- It automatically discovers and adds all tables from a connection to a relational data source as assets in the catalog.

- It uploads files to the dedicated, encrypted cloud object-storage bucket that's associated with the catalog.

- It includes an object-storage instance to store assets that are copied into the catalog.

After adding data assets to a catalog, data stewards can alter the assets' profiles to add generated metadata about the data assets' contents, and in addition, data scientists and developers can enrich assets by having catalog collaborators add ratings and reviews. Catalog collaborators can also create tags that describe different assets while making sure data classes accurately define the type of data stored within the assets—all while having set business terms that help describe data in a standard way for an enterprise. Data catalogs can also help control access to data policies. Policies should apply to all catalogs within an enterprise, and the corresponding policy tools should be available only to users who have special permissions within the catalog. Policy tools should enable an organization to:

- Create business terms that describe what data to use in policies

- Write policies to deny access and protect sensitive data assets

- Write policies to mask data values in columns that contain sensitive data and monitor trends in policy enforcement over time

Data catalogs must maintain data discovery records that show which collaborators need access to certain assets and corresponding information in data sets from across an entire organization, without needing separate credentials for every source. This creates a single platform where any member of an enterprise can locate the data they're authorized to access. To ensure security, the data catalog assigns the correct roles to its users based on their needs and places the necessary restrictions on what the user can and can't do inside the catalog. Types of collaborators and their functions potentially include:

- Authors: Subject-matter experts who will pull and draft the appropriate information into the catalog

- Approvers: Analysts who can review, comment, approve, or deny the delivered information once authors have completed their draft

- Publishers: Personnel authorized to make public within the catalog the approved information and make the new business terms and data assets available to anyone with access to the business glossary

To help transform large amounts of raw data into consumable, quality information that's ready for analysis, a data catalog should have self-service preparation features to support any data preparation solution the enterprise already has in place. The following features of a catalog should make it easy to explore, prepare, and deliver data that can be trusted and used across a business:

- Powerful operations that clean, organize, fix, and validate data

- Scripting support for the efficient and flexible manipulation of data

- Scheduling and monitoring of data preparation flows

- Profiles for validating data

- Visualizations for gaining insight into data

- Enforcement of policies that mask data

- Support for unstructured data

A catalog helps alleviate manual processes and dependencies with advanced discovery capabilities typically driven by ML and semantic context. This makes it easier to find relevant assets quickly and at scale. Ways in which a catalog enables data discovery include:

- Search keywords and filters based on subject tags and other asset properties

- Preview capabilities to ensure that users are selecting the correct data asset

- Access reviews about assets created by collaborators within the catalog to help identify the best assets from which to pull

- Access asset recommendations that are automatically compiled based on usage history, similar assets, and other factors

Consider the benefits when a business has a properly implemented data catalog:

- Decreased time to results with more time to analyze data and put it to use

- Ability to capture contextual asset knowledge and improve data's utility

- Ability to track data lineage and improve trust in data quality

- Capability of marketing information assets for broader consumption

- Assistance with data governance and compliance

In contrast, when a business does not have a data catalog or has one that is implemented incorrectly, there is the:

- Likelihood of wasted time while searching and tagging data

- Possibility of losing crucial knowledge when users locate data but can't find colleagues who understand the data

- Possibility of losing knowledge of who has access to data

- Threat of failure to meet compliance and governance requirements

Using a Data Catalog to Improve Business Taxonomy

Understanding these practical benefits of a modern data catalog is just a beginning. It's equally important to understand how to start integrating it into any business to realize value faster. When the goal of an organization is to increase efficiency and collaboration across stakeholders, the first place on which to focus improvements should be the company's business taxonomy (its custom vocabulary for discussing functions and processes). This will become the foundation for content categorization and data relationships, and it will provide a guideline that improves the speed at which data can be found, accessed, or reused, as shown in Figure 6.1.

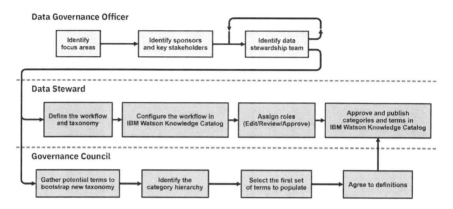

Figure 6.1: Data citizens must work together to build a business taxonomy that benefits their organization as a whole

Best practices when establishing a robust business taxonomy include the following four steps:

Step 1: Focus on a single high-value information area.

As opposed to trying to organize all assets at once, it's far more efficient to focus on a particular segment of the business that will drive the greatest impact, and then organize those assets first. For instance, if compliance and regulatory processes, such as those required to comply with the EU's General Data Protection Regulation (GDPR) or the California Consumer Privacy Act (CCPA), are high priority for an organization, begin with establishing terms and classifying assets related to personally identifiable information (PII).

Step 2: Concentrate on the meaning of business definitions.

Use the language of a particular industry in the form of logical or BI models to power existing terms and standards already set in place. Take time to understand how the organization applies certain concepts and definitions in its business operations, and then build the catalog specific to these key components, data types, and common uses of data. (The catalog will be extended and expanded to encompass other components and data types as additional projects are undertaken, but leave that for a later step.)

Step 3: Establish benefits and encourage interest within the organization.

Although adoption of a business taxonomy might not happen overnight, it is critical for an organization to understand the advantage of having a single place of information storage. Within a specific sector of a business, champion the idea of selecting a focused area to start integrating a data catalog with an established business taxonomy so that the organization can provide the example of its data being consolidated in one place.

Step 4: Develop and commit to milestones.

The final step is to establish official milestones to which the organization commits itself for implementation of the business categories, business terms, and correct assignment of user roles—and moreover the data catalog process. Whether there is a mature DataOps culture in place or this is the first step, it is important to remember that within each organization, the stakeholders in and out of IT need to add value to drive success of data projects.

Figure 6.1 above shows how different roles within an organization should combine efforts to develop a business taxonomy. Depending on the size of an organization, the roles of data governance officer, data steward, and governance council may vary and overlap. The figure shown is often representative of large enterprises.

7

Common Use Cases for a Data Fabric

Several use cases based on events at actual but unnamed companies illustrate ways in which any organization can successfully leverage a data fabric in different scenarios.

Use Case 1: Driving Simpler Cloud Integration

Modern enterprises are struggling with increasingly complex data real estates as data becomes more diverse, distributed, and dynamic across hybrid cloud environments. New data sources, applications, and requirements are multiplying. As architectures get more complicated, it's harder to maintain them and provide access to the data needed, which can lead to large percentages of data being overlooked or underused within an enterprise.

Multicloud data integration addresses this complexity and sprawl across on-premises, multicloud, and hybrid cloud environments. When used as part of a data fabric, data integration can turn a siloed data architecture into one where the right data is delivered to the right place at the right time.

Data fabric technology provides automated data governance and privacy controls while maintaining regulatory compliance, no matter where data resides. It also builds the basis for 360-degree customer intelligence and trustworthy AI.

Modern data integration solutions that are part of a data fabric enable creation of flexible, reusable, augmented data pipelines that can help users create and deliver data products across diverse domains and lines of businesses. As organizations adapt to the complexities of the modern data landscape, Chief Data Officers (CDOs), Chief Information Officers (CIOs), and other data leaders often struggle with the management and integration of data while ensuring its quality and governance. According to the IBM Institute for Business Value (IBV) study cited earlier, data integration with multiple systems of records is executives' "top implementation challenge to a digital experience platform," and 40 percent of respondents cited siloed data sources and lack of sharing as organizational barriers.

In contrast, a sound multicloud data integration strategy can:

- Democratize data access by delivering data where the enterprise needs it, whether it be on-premises or any cloud, in near real-time, batch, or a virtualized manner

- Provide real-time synchronization of operational and analytic data stores without disrupting or impacting mission-critical data

- Serve the ever-growing population of new data consumers by providing access to data, wherever it resides, in a controlled, regulated manner

- Reduce vendor lock-in and enable greater choice in data environments, empowering enterprises to make selections that meet their unique combination of pricing, performance, security, and compliance requirements

The goal of multicloud data integration is to democratize data access across the enterprise, enable continuous availability for mission-critical data, and empower new data consumers. At the same time, the enterprise must remain true to secure, governed, and performant principles regarding its data. Modern data integration solutions require a data delivery platform that supports different integration and delivery styles while using knowledge graphs, active metadata, and policy enforcements to unify and govern data across a distributed landscape. By leveraging a flexible architecture that is purpose-built for cloud native workloads, and infusing ML-powered capabilities that enable consumers to unlock insight from their data, modern data integration solutions can provide faster access to high-quality data for downstream analytics, BI, AI, and data-intensive application consumers.

Data integration helps combine structured and unstructured data from disparate sources into meaningful and valuable data sets. Integration styles such as bulk/batch integration. For example, either the Extract, Transform, Load (ETL) or Extract, Load, Transform (ELT) processes, data replication and streaming integration, change data capture, and data virtualization all enable a variety of integration use cases.

- ETL and ELT are both data integration processes that move raw data from a source system to a target data repository, such as a data lake or data warehouse. Advanced transformation of the data can be applied either in-flight (ETL) or post-load (ELT). Data sources can be in multiple repositories, including legacy systems or systems of record, which are then transferred using bulk or batch integration to a target data location.

- Data replication provides the flexibility to copy data between a variety of heterogeneous sources and targets for dynamic delivery, making it ideal for multisite workload distribution and continuous availability—whether across data centers, from on-premises, or to the cloud.

- Change data capture records database changes as they happen in real-time and delivers them to target databases, message queues, or as part of an ETL solution.

- Data virtualization connects data across data sources and makes it accessible through a single access point—regardless of data location, size, type, or format. Data engineers can quickly and easily fulfill ad hoc data integration requests to validate hypotheses or what-if scenarios.

Data cataloging can help users find and use the right data with a rich and metadata-driven index of cataloged assets. Data catalogs with built-in quality analysis can make inferences and identify anomalies. Some catalogs have built-in refineries that help with data discovery, cleansing and transforming the data with data shaping (changing data in format or context) operations.

Data governance makes the right data easier to find for those who should have access to it, while keeping sensitive data hidden or masked. A governance framework designed to automate the enforcement of data protection policies and backed by automated metadata tagging is ideal for the establishment and enforcement of data governance policies and rules.

Advanced data engineering automates data access and sharing, accelerating data delivery with active metadata. Enterprises can also use orchestration to make DataOps pipelines simpler to build and run, improving the integration and communication of data flows between data producers and data consumers. Automatic workload balancing and elastic scaling make jobs ready for any environment and any data volume. Finally, data cataloging can include solutions that provide self-service access, the ability to query all data, and continuous data availability.

Organizations using a data fabric will be able to dynamically connect, optimize, and automate data management processes and reduce the time it takes to integrate data, making for a more agile environment.

Multi-Cloud Data Integration

Multi-Cloud Data Integration (MCDI) is the holistic set of capabilities that enable clients to connect to, refine, and deliver data, wherever it resides. Organizations need comprehensive capabilities enabling decentralization of data architectures so they are not forced to focus on just one single warehouse or one cloud effort to make their analytics and AI successful. They need the ability to unlock the value of their data while keeping true to secure, governed, and performant principles. A proper data integration tool has functionality spanning batch ETL/ELT, data replication, messaging, data virtualization, and streaming/real-time capabilities.

Hybrid cloud is driving the need for more sophisticated data integration. Organizations are demanding cloud-native, cloud-first sets of services that help clients start or progress their data and AI journeys. As the market shifts to organizations using cloud data warehousing for cheaper compute and store, vendors need to focus on delivering a set of extensive capabilities that let organizations pair the optimal integration style with the right type of data delivery. Enterprises need ways to build intelligent data pipelines that are all-encompassing of complex transformations, data validation, data cleansing, enrichment, and deep enforcement of policies to unlock tight analytics.

Some Key Use Cases for Data Fabric MCDI

For Data Fabric MCDI, there are four prototypical key use cases. The intent of these use cases is to provide clear entry points that resonate with organizations to help them start small and focus on specific, targeted problems. Enabling clients to be successful on these use cases will strengthen their ability to take real steps towards a data fabric architecture.

The first case involves multiple goals: directly ingesting data into the data fabric, providing continuous availability for mission-critical data, building fully governed data pipelines, delivering data-science-ready data, and delivering data as a service for a specific line of business. Data ingestion uses the main services of data virtualization, data integration, data quality, data staging, and replication. Expected benefits include being able to use ELT or ETL pipelines to facilitate a shift of data to a cloud data warehouse, enable ground-to-cloud and cloud-to-cloud migration and synchronization, assess data at the time of ingestion, and provide the ability to use event-driven architecture and publish/subscribe relationships, and ensure interoperability with streams and events. The continuous availability goal uses replication services and seeks to support discovery of a "replica" relationship between assets and provide user-defined availability SLAs and policies for data assets.

Second, the goal of building fully governed data pipelines uses the main services of intelligent knowledge catalogs, data integration, data quality, data staging, data virtualization, and replication. Expected benefits include providing the ability for support data engineers to construct and operationalize data pipelines via DataOps methodology, supporting economy of API functions to let clients build on top of integration capabilities, and pushdown optimization. Additional benefits include the ability to automate and orchestrate remediation of data quality and the advantage of being able to trust data with automated lineage support.

Third, the goal of delivering data-science-ready data uses the main services of data integration, data quality, data staging, data refining, and data virtualization. The major benefit is the ability to orchestrate delivery of data to data-science tooling for ML use cases.

And fourth is Data as a Service (DaaS) for a line of business uses the main services of Business Intelligence (BI), forecasting, and planning analytics. Some expected benefits include gaining a complete picture of the enterprise and understanding what's next by automatically unifying business data to gain actionable insights, as well as gaining the ability to deliver dynamic, reliable plans, budgets, and forecasts with speed, and adjust plans as the market changes to optimize outcomes with built-in predictive analytics and AI capabilities. Additional benefits include the ability to enable finance teams to automate, accelerate, and simplify the financial close process with minimal IT support, to manage audit compliance, as well as to enable an AI-fueled BI that supports the entire analytics cycle, from discovery to operationalization.

Use Case 2: Going 360 Degrees

According to a survey of 3,000 CEOs by the IBV, improving the customer experience is the number one business priority of the highest-performing enterprise organizations. Realizing this goal includes taking advantage of analytics for hyper-personalization and next-best-offers, while infusing compliance, privacy, and fraud identification capabilities for better overall customer care. Accomplishing this relies on a simplified, governed single view of a customer across multiple data sources.

To help achieve this, a data fabric architecture helps ensure quality data can be accessed by the right people at the right time. A data fabric architecture needs to provide a strong foundation for 360-degree customer intelligence, enabling a customer-centric approach with multicloud data integration, data governance and compliance, and MLOps capabilities (a set of practices that aims to deploy and maintain machine-learning models in production reliably and efficiently). Having a 360-degree view of customers is essential because whether an organization operates in a business-to-business (B2B) or business-to-consumer (B2C) environment, their customers expect them to be knowledgeable about their needs and history during every interaction. All touchpoints must provide consistent, well-informed service. Traditionally, this has been difficult to achieve due to the scattered and siloed nature of many organizations' data, but embracing a customer-360 approach with a data fabric has the potential to unlock new opportunities.

Organizations are looking to use the data they already have, bringing in data of different types from a variety of sources to capture a complete understanding of individual clients and customers. The goal is to retain and grow existing customer bases or to convert prospects to customers, adding value to the varying conversations and touchpoints the customer has, all while using analytics to speak and target intelligently. The challenge, then, is how to connect all that data in such a way that organizations have robust, high-quality insight available to attract each individual customer at every touchpoint, while also balancing compliance requirements. A customer-360 approach is the answer.

Creating this all-important 360-degree view requires breaking down silos to develop an integrated view of all that data in near real-time and put it in a state ready for analytics. Doing so will help an organization apply AI and automated analytics (rather than search for data), augmenting knowledge about their customers across their environments. This way, organizations won't be just collecting data, but rather connecting data to create a complete customer profile. This connection instead of collection across data types and sources (including data marts, warehouses, CRM systems, and other data stores) can help create a self-service, ready-for-analytics view of the customer. It creates a customer view that's high-quality and easily accessible—but only by those who should have access. Only then is it ready for use in the analytics and AI models that will be needed to inform customer interactions.

It is critical that organizations be able to bring together disparate data into a single 360-degree view of their customers and processes to provide a basis for users to collaborate and innovate. Customer 360-degree solutions help build these more insightful views of customers at scale, for better self-service and data stewardship.

At the heart of a customer 360-degree solution is data governance, which provides a singular view of business entities (customer, product, account, and other attributes) as well as application and data resources, typically stored and potentially duplicated across siloed applications. Governance helps achieve customer-centricity or product-centricity by providing that trusted 360-degree view of organizational data that facilitates the capabilities of finding, reconciling, and consuming data, as well as identifying relationships within context across a variety of use cases.

In addition to governance, automation helps to resolve multiple siloed records to a customer entity, and this simplification for analytics, machine-learning (ML), or customer care enables self-service access by which business users can achieve accelerated insights, customer personalization, and compliance. This automation across connected sources brings timely, quality data to downstream applications, such as customer-care applications, helping to bring the customer 360-degree view to action.

The components need to develop a 360-degree view include:

- Data preparation and connection: Connecting and transforming raw data into data that's ready for matching across multiple data sets, using a self-service data preparation and/or ETL tool

- Data matching: Automapping customer attributes for an intelligent matching algorithm that users can tune and train to deliver a trusted, unified source of customer data

- Entity resolution (the process that resolves entities and detects relationships): The pipelines perform entity resolution as they process incoming identity records in three phases: recognize, resolve, and relate.

- Data cataloging: A catalog tool that lets an organization access, curate, categorize, and share data, knowledge assets, and their relationships

- Data virtualization: The process that enables a single view across multiple silos without data movement, connecting key sources of customer data at the time of analysis, saving time through self-service access and removing the need for complex data pipelines

- Data visualization: The ability to understand the quality and distribution of data and transform that data to be ready for analytics

By connecting key sources of customer data at the time of analysis, rather than re-collecting it, organizations can save time and money with self-service empowerment of end users. With data governance capabilities integrated within a data fabric, organizations can deliver a comprehensive customer view that delivers value with the highest levels of service. The data fabric approach aims to deliver integrated yet modular capabilities to provide automation, augmentation, and agility in implementing several data fabric use cases, including customer-360, customer intelligence, analytics for upsell/cross-sell, targeted marketing, fraud detection, risk analytics, real-time analytics, operational insights, and analytics and insights in specific industry verticals. The Data Fabric for Customer 360 entry point, for example, is about giving marketers and other analysts the ability to build the view they want, from the sources of customer data that are relevant, without having to get in line at the IT queue to get a result.

Use Case 3: True Enterprise Governance

In addition to providing a strong foundation for multicloud data integration, 360-degree customer intelligence, and trustworthy AI, the data governance and privacy capability of a data fabric strengthens compliance with automated governance and privacy controls, while maintaining regulatory compliance no matter where data resides. Strong governance makes the right quality data easier to find for those who should have access to it, while keeping sensitive data hidden unless appropriate. Giving an enterprise insights into its business and customers is a competitive advantage. Insight-driven businesses are more likely to have a strong data governance strategy, have an executive in charge of their data governance, use AI, and embed data stewardship throughout the organization.

Strong privacy parameters help increase readiness for compliance and data protection anywhere, on-premises or across hybrid clouds. These parameters enable businesses to understand and apply industry-specific regulatory policies and governance rules on data.

As organizations strive to establish cultures of data-driven decision-making, the ability to rely on quality data that is compliant with a dynamic regulatory environment is critical. Such an approach helps organizations deal with several critical challenges.

First is the need for privacy at scale. The risks of noncompliance (such as legal penalties, loss of customer trust, and loss of reputation) are real. More than 60 jurisdictions around the world have enacted or proposed privacy and data protection laws. Most companies worldwide will face a need for compliance with at least one privacy-focused data protection regulation. Rather than responding to each challenge individually, a proactive approach to privacy and data protection is an opportunity for organizations to build customer trust. To do it, data leaders need to build a holistic privacy program across the organization.

Second is the need to improve data access. Secure data-sharing is a crucial factor when multiple teams require access to enterprise data. That data must be traceable and visible only to those who are authorized to use it. Yet for many organizations, securing data that moves across multiple cloud and on-premises environments remains a challenge. Without being able to ensure compliance at scale and from one environment to another, teams hesitate to share data between business units, thereby deepening silos. This causes IT teams to have to protect and ensure each data repository on an individual basis and can lead to groups spinning up their own repositories (shadow IT), which only leads to more complexity.

Third is the need to maintain data-quality standards across the organization. Only a small percent of business executives trust the data they receive. Every year, poor data quality can cost organizations millions of dollars. For all users throughout an organization to be able to fully understand and have confidence in the data they are about to use, a data governance foundation of business definitions and metadata is essential. This foundation includes business terms, data classifications, reference data, associated metadata, and the establishment and enforcement of data governance policies and rules.

Fourth is the need for data lineage and traceability. Once analytics teams have built and deployed data products (such as dashboards, reports, and ML models), they need to be able to look back and see where the data product came from. For auditability and compliance use cases (most often in regulated industries), an analytics team may be required to show all the steps taken in the life of the data as it has been transformed from the transactional system where it was originally created into its final form as it is used to support business decision-making. And for end users, being able to see the data sources and transformations can save a great deal of time as they build their own customized version of the dashboard.

Fifth is the need to facilitate data consumption. To leverage the innovative and disruptive power of data, enterprises need to enable self-service data consumption. The ability to simplify data access and consumption is predicated on a robust framework and architecture that ensures data users in an organization can find and use the right data through a rich and metadata-driven index of cataloged assets. Data governance and privacy proactively enables enterprises to satisfy the need to drive innovation and meet business outcomes.

All these factors drive a sixth need: data cataloging. The quality of an organization's data determines how confidently it can act on insights. If low-quality data goes into AI models, it could lead to inaccurate, noncompliant, or discriminatory results. Getting the best insights means being able to access data that is fresh, clean, and relevant, with a consistent taxonomy. A data catalog can help users easily find and use the right data with a rich and metadata-driven index of cataloged assets.

Building Blocks for Data Governance

Ultimately, the goal of governance is knowing where data comes from, what it is, who can access it, and when it should be retired. Several key technology building blocks exist to meet the need to integrate and improve data privacy, access, quality, and traceability for all the data in an organization.

Metadata tracks the origin, privacy level, age, and potential uses of enterprise data. Manually generating metadata is cumbersome, but with ML, data can be intelligently tagged with metadata (automated metadata generation) to mitigate human error and "dark data" (data that is acquired through various computer network operations but not used in any manner to derive insights or for decision-making). Automatic tagging of the metadata enables policy enforcement at the point of access so that sensitive data can be used in a nonidentifiable and compliant way. In addition, metadata can establish a common vocabulary of business terms that provide context to data and facilitate linking data from different sources. This context adds semantic meaning to data so that it becomes more findable, usable, and consistent within the organization, a key factor when seeking data for analytics and AI.

Automated governance of data access and lineage is another building block. Data lineage shows how data has been accessed and used and by whom. Knowing where data comes from is useful not only for compliance reporting but also for building trustworthy and explainable AI models. This process can be automated without complicating access. With restrictions built directly into access points, only the data that users are authorized to access will be visible. Additionally, sensitive data can be dynamically masked so that models and data sets can be shared without exposing private data to unauthorized users. This clarity around what data can and can't be used supports self-service data demands and enables organizations to be nimble in responding to line-of-business needs.

Data virtualization connects data across all locations and makes the disparate data sources appear as a single database. This can help organizations ensure compliant access to the data through governed data access without moving it. Using the single virtualized governed layer, user access to data is defined in one place instead of at each source, reducing complexity of access management. This is discussed in more detail elsewhere in this book.

Enterprises must comply with a wide variety of changing regulations that differ according to geography, industry, and data type. These regulations need to be broken down into a catalog of requirements with a clear set of actions that businesses must take. Regulatory information should be automatically ingested, deduplicated, and applied to workflows.

An organization's data privacy and governance requirements need to seamlessly integrate across the set of current (and future) business opportunities or drivers. To help achieve this, an organization should develop and adopt a global data strategy, as well as an open and holistic data and technology architecture so that technology components and data assets can be better managed and governed.

Employing a robust governance and privacy capability is dependent on a technology stack that is designed to gain end-to-end governance, deliver quality data, and ultimately accelerate collaboration. In the context of an enterprise, the value of data governance is amplified when this capability is integrated with data integration, providing a comprehensive view of clients and enabling maximum data utilization to drive business outcomes.

As part of a modern data fabric, the data governance and privacy capabilities create an end-to-end user experience rooted in metadata and active policy management that lets users view, access, manipulate, and analyze data without the need to understand its physical format or location, and without having to move or copy it.

The technology components needed in the data fabric approach facilitates the ability of companies to automatically apply industry-specific regulatory policies and rules to their data assets, securing across the enterprise. This should include:

- An AI-augmented data catalog that helps business users easily understand, collaborate on, enrich, and access the right data

- A metadata and governance layer for all data, analytics, and AI initiatives that helps increase visibility and collaboration on any cloud

- The ability to dynamically and consistently mask data at a user-defined granular level

- The ability to create anonymized training data and test sets while maintaining data integrity

Governance is a journey and is constantly evolving to meet government and industry requirements as well as the unique or custom needs of each individual organization. Such a dynamic environment must facilitate policy adaptations for users involved with security, administration, compliance, and other forms of governance. The data fabric and catalog become essential components in enabling these users to create their own models and score them as part of the governance process.

Use Case 4: Toward Trustworthy, Transparent AI

In an era where trust has become of tremendous importance to customers, every organization has a responsibility to adhere to ethical, explainable AI practices that respect individual rights, privacy, and nondiscrimination. When enterprises establish trust in their AI systems, revenues and customer satisfaction increase, time to market shrinks, and competitive positioning improves. However, when this is overlooked, trust for the organization can erode and result in failed audits and regulatory fines resulting in the loss of brand reputation and revenues. Success in building, deploying, and managing AI/ML models is based on trusted data and automated data science tools and processes, and this requires a technology platform that can orchestrate data of many types and sources within hybrid multicloud environments. Data fabric's technology architecture approach helps ensure that the right people can access quality data at the right time no matter where it resides.

Data fabric provides a strong foundation for MLOps and trustworthy AI. In addition, data fabric enables multicloud data integration, data governance and compliance, and 360-degree customer intelligence.

Well-planned, executed, and controlled AI that is built to mitigate risks and drive desired analytic outcomes requires building trust in the data, models, and processes.

Strength and trust in AI outcomes require a connection to data that is accurate, of high quality, and ready for self-service consumption by the right stakeholders. AI model strength depends on the ability to aggregate both structured and unstructured data from disparate internal and external sources, whether from on-premises, public clouds, or private clouds. Successful data collection and usage hinges on establishing fairness in training data, tracking its lineage, and ensuring data privacy when offering self-service analysis by multiple personas.

To ensure transparency and accountability at each stage of the model lifecycle, MLOps-automated, integrated data science tools help to operationalize the building, deployment, and monitoring of AI models. MLOps increases the efficiency for continuous integration, delivery, and deployment of workflows to help mitigate bias, risk, and drift for more-accurate data-driven decisions. Some unique MLOps implementations also infuse the AI model process with fairness, substantiation, and robustness.

Across the model lifecycle, from model building through monitoring, lack of automated processes can lead to inconsistency, inefficiency, and lack of transparency. AI governance provides trusted automation that drives consistent, repeatable processes that can decrease time to production, increase model transparency, ensure traceability, and drive AI at scale. Models and algorithms are only as good as the data used to create them. Data may be incomplete or biased, which can lead to inaccurate algorithms and analytic outcomes. A method of tying these sources together is vital. Data scientists, analysts, and developers need self-service data access to the most appropriate data for their project. Setting up privacy controls for multiple personas, providing real-time access to authorized data users, and tracking data lineage can be challenging without the right tools.

Data cleansing and prepping can be a very manual process and is often one of the most time-consuming and least enjoyable tasks for data scientists. Most would prefer to spend their time mining or modeling data. A data fabric solution needs to able to automate these tasks as part the ML lifecycle to accelerate time-to-value. A common complaint among data scientists is the lack of integrated tools for cleansing and preparing data and for building, deploying, scaling, and training models. The tedious task of using multiple standalone tools is often coupled with the lack of software documentation, FAQs, and use cases for those tools. The lack of integrated tools can lead to governance and compliance issues. Once a model is built, collaboration between the model builder and other teams, including software engineering, AI operations, and business analysts, is imperative. Building an automated structure to do this in a timely manner is key.

Once a model is deployed, it's imperative to continually measure and monitor the model's performance. Changes can result from model degradation, drift, bias, and other causes. Using manual processes to detect these changes can lead to costly inaccuracies and lack of governance, resulting in regulatory consequences and customer mistrust. Automating the process of monitoring and retraining models as well as collecting model facts across the lifecycle drives consistency and transparency, automatically addressing model fairness and regulatory requirements.

Having previously defined the need to build trust in data, models, and processes, organizations need to leverage automation at each stage of the AI lifecycle. A set of technology building blocks are needed at each stage to establish well-planned, -executed, and -controlled AI. Organizations need to be able to automatically capture metadata across the model development lifecycle to facilitate subsequent enterprise validation or external regulation. Model Risk Governance (MRG) can help facilitate end-to-end AI governance for risk and compliance by using workflows that let users set up their own custom steps and processes. As shown earlier by the interrelationships between corporate roles in Figure 6.1, data custodians and users must cooperate to establish synchronization of information and facts about models with deployment metadata so these functions can be properly automated. That way, MRG enables model validators, risk analysts, and business users make informed decisions about an AI model and its lifecycle faster. MRG should facilitate the creation of model entries, which are essentially model use cases that can be created by a data science leader or model owner. Once data scientists have finished developing the model and have automatically captured model facts, they should be able to add the model to the model entry and view its facts as well.

In summary, organizations with a vested interest in data fabric technology are seeking a wide range of capabilities that include:

- A way to integrate data of many types and sources across diverse deployments

- Self-service access with privacy controls and a way to track lineage

- Automated model building, deployment, scaling, training, and monitoring

- Automated governance and risk management to help ensure data quality and regulatory compliance

Use Case 5: Data Observability

"Data observability" is the blanket term for understanding the health and the state of data in a knowledge system. Essentially, data observability covers an umbrella of activities and technologies that, when combined, facilitate identification, troubleshooting, and resolution of data issues in near real-time. By encompassing a basket of activities, observability is much more useful for engineers. Unlike the data quality frameworks and tools that came out along with the concept of the data warehouse, observability doesn't stop at describing the problem. It provides enough context to enable the engineer to resolve the problem and start conversations to prevent that type of error from occurring again. The way to achieve this is to pull best practices from DevOps and apply them to Data Operations.

Data observability is the natural evolution of the data-quality movement, and it's making Data Operations as a practice very challenging. The

DataOps cycle outlines the fundamental activities that need to occur to improve the way data is managed within the DataOps workflow. This cycle consists of three distinct stages: detection, awareness, and iteration.

The detection stage of the DataOps cycle is validation-focused. It includes the same data-quality checks that have been used since the inception of the data warehouse. Essentially, someone is charged with making sure the business rules are being applied and adhered to for all data sets that are coming into the system. The data-quality framework that lives in the detection stage is important but reactionary by its very nature. It provides the ability to know whether the data that's already stored in a lake or warehouse is in the expected form.

It's also important to know if established tools and procedures are following established rules for validating data sets. Lack of insight into the causes of issues makes it almost impossible to establish new business rules for engineers to follow as circumstances change over time. This realization is fueling the demand for "shift left" awareness (sharing of information with personnel closer to the customer than data custodians customarily are) of data issues and the development of data observability tools that make this possible.

Awareness is a visibility-focused stage of the DataOps phase. This is where the conversation around data governance comes into the picture and introduces a metadata-first approach. Centralizing and standardizing pipeline and data set metadata across an organization gives teams visibility into issues that happen within the entire organization. The centralization of metadata is crucial to giving the entire organization awareness into the end-to-end health of its data. By doing this, the organization moves to a more proactive approach to solving data issues. If there is bad data in the "domain," someone can trace the error to a certain point in the system upstream. Awareness means data engineering team A can go on to look at data engineering team B's pipelines, be able to understand what is going on there, and collaborate with them to potentially fix the issue. Similarly, data engineering team B can detect an issue and trace what impact it will have downstream. Data engineering team A will know that an issue can happen and take whatever measures are necessary to contain it.

This is the biggest area that has been lacking in DataOps. Not only is there now a universal language that all teams can point to and discuss with each other, but data teams can share this information with stakeholders and help them understand what they plan to do and how they intend to support the data that the stakeholders need, as well as rectify any other issues anyone encounters. In the iteration stage, teams focus on data-as-code. This stage of the cycle is process-focused. Teams are making sure that they have repeatable and sustainable standards that will be applied to all data development to ensure that the result will be the same trustworthy data at the end of the pipelines. In this way, the gradual improvement of the data platform's overall health is facilitated by the detection of issues, awareness into any upstream root causes, and efficient processes for iteration.

With iteration, teams focus on data-as-code. This stage of the cycle is process-focused. Teams are ensuring that they have repeatable and sustainable standards that will be applied to all of our data development to ensure that we get the same trustworthy data at the end of those pipelines. The gradual improvement of the data platform's overall health is made possible by the detection of issues, awareness of the upstream root causes, and efficient processes for iteration.

Data Observability Capabilities

The data observability function needs to include these activities:

- Monitoring: Using a dashboard that provides an operational view of a pipeline or system

- Alerting: Must cover both expected events and anomalies

- Tracking: The ability to set and track specific events

- Comparisons: Monitoring over time, with alerts for anomalies

- Analysis: Automated issue detection that adapts to the organizational pipeline and data health

- Logging: A record of an event in a standardized format for faster resolution

- SLA tracking: The ability to measure data quality and pipeline metadata against predefined standards

The difference between these activities and those that data teams already do lies in how these activities fit into the end-to-end data operations workflow and the level of context they provide on data issues. For most organizations, observability is siloed. Teams collect metadata on the pipelines they own. Different teams may be collecting metadata that may not connect to critical downstream or upstream events. More importantly, that metadata isn't visualized or reported on a dashboard that can be viewed across teams. There may be standardized logging policies for one team but not for another, and there's no way for other teams to easily access them. Some teams may run algorithms on data sets to ensure they are meeting business rules, but the team that builds the pipelines doesn't have a way to monitor how the data is transforming within that pipeline and whether it will be delivered in a form the consumers expect. The list of pitfalls is long.

Without the ability to standardize and centralize these activities, teams can't have the level of awareness they need to proactively iterate their data platform. A downstream data team can't trace the source of its issues upstream, and an upstream data team can't improve its processes without having visibility into downstream dependencies. The operational and data set health monitoring step involves getting visibility into the enterprise's operational and data set health. It's the foundation for any data observability framework. Monitoring data set health refers to monitoring a data set as a whole. When data is in a static location, it's referred to as "data at rest." Monitoring data at rest answers questions such as these:

- Did this data set arrive on time?

- Is this data set being updated as frequently as it needs to be?

- Is the expected volume of data available in this data set?

In contrast, "data in motion" refers to data when it's moving through pipelines. Operational monitoring focuses on the state of such pipelines. This type of monitoring provides awareness into the state of data while it's transforming and moving through pipelines. This type of monitoring answers questions such as these:

- How does pipeline performance affect the data set quality?

- Under what conditions is a run considered successful?

- What operations are transforming the data set before it reaches the lake or warehouse?

While data set and data pipeline monitoring are usually separated into two distinct activities, it's important to keep them conceptually coupled together to achieve a solid foundation of observability. These two states are highly interconnected and dependent on each other. Separating these two activities into silos where different teams may be using different tools to observe them makes it more difficult to get a high-level view of an organization's data health.

Column-level profiling (the determination of statistical information about distribution of data values and the associated patterns assigned to each data attribute) is key to overcoming this hierarchy. Column-level profiling, once a solid foundation has been laid for it, provides the necessary insights to establish new business rules and enforce existing ones. That level of awareness can help an organization improve its data-quality framework in an actionable way. This level of observability helps the enterprise answer questions such as these:

- What is the expected range for a column?

- What is the expected schema of this column?

- How unique is this column?

The next stage is "row-level validation," which looks at the values in each row and checks that they are accurate. This type of observability looks at questions such as these:

- Are the values in each row in the expected form?

- Are the values the exact length they are expected to be?

- Given the context, is there enough information here to be useful to the end user?

A lot of organizations get tunnel vision on row-level validation, but that's just mistaking the trees for the forest. By building an observability framework starting with operational and data set monitoring, an organization can get big-picture context on its data platform's health while still being able to home in on the root cause of issues and their impact downstream.

Implementing a Data Observability Framework

Let's bring this full circle. Data observability is a collection of activities and technologies that help an organization understand the health and the state of data within its system. Data observability is a byproduct of the DataOps movement, and it has been the missing piece for making agile, iterative improvements to many enterprises' data products possible. Data observability isn't a silver bullet, and neither is DataOps. Technology alone will not solve all data problems. The best monitoring dashboards report on all metadata and are equipped with the most powerful automation and algorithms, but they are only good for the pipelines each individual group owns, unless there is universal organization adoption. Conversely, everyone can be bought into DataOps as a practice, but if the technology to support it isn't present, it's just a nice-to-have documentation philosophy that doesn't impact output.

So how should an enterprise implement a data observability framework that can improve end-to-end data quality? What metrics should the organization be tracking at each stage? The organization needs a high-functioning data observability framework that includes the following attributes:

- A DataOps culture

- A standardized data platform

- A unified data-observability platform

Before an organization considers thinking about producing a high-value data product, it needs to undertake mass adoption of a DataOps culture, which essentially means treating every aspect of data as an asset. Everyone needs to buy into this, particularly leadership, because those are the enterprise roles that dictate the systems and processes for development, maintenance, and feedback. As powerful as a bottom-up movement can be, top-down budget approvals are necessary to make the technological changes needed to support a DataOps system.

Once organizational teams have bought into the idea of being efficiently data-oriented, leadership can move the organization toward a standardized data platform. Organizationally, this means that in order to achieve end-to-end ownership and accountability across all teams, these things are needed:

- An IA infrastructure in place that will enable teams to speak the same language and openly communicate about issues
- Standardized libraries for API and data management (e.g., querying data warehouses, reading/writing from data lakes, pulling data from APIs)
- Standardized library for data quality
- Source code tracking, data versioning, and CI/CD processes in place
- A unified observability platform that gives the organization open access to data about the system's health

This observability platform acts as a centralized metadata repository. It encompasses all the features previously mentioned (e.g., monitoring, alerting, tracking, comparison, analysis) that can give data teams an end-to-end view of how the sections of the platform they own are affecting other sections. For operational health, organizations should be collecting execution metadata. This includes metadata on pipeline states, duration, delays, retries, and times between subsequent runs. For data set monitoring, organizations should be looking at the completeness of each data set, the availability, the volume of data in and out, and schema changes. For column-level profiling, organizations should collect summary statistics on columns and use anomaly detection to alert personnel of changes. It would need to look at Mean, Max, Min trends within columns. For row-level validation, organizations should be ensuring the previous checks didn't fail at the row level and that all personnel are following business rules. This is contextual, so organizations will have to use their discretion.

In summary, data observability is the backbone of any data team's ability to be agile and to iterate its products. Without observability, a team cannot rely on its infrastructure or tools because errors can't be tracked down quickly enough. This leads to less agility in building new features and improvements for customers, which means organizations are essentially throwing away money by not investing in this key piece of the DataOps framework.

8

Two Cornerstones of a Data Fabric

This chapter more closely examines data catalogs, examines the value of data virtualization, and shows why these two technologies form two important cornerstones in a data fabric approach and architecture.

Examples of the Value of a Data Catalog

Leveraging a data catalog can help an organization accomplish the levels of success that it needs to meet due to the ever-increasing demands placed on data-centric businesses. From ensuring that an enterprise can meet compliance regulations, to facilitating data lake governance, or to cutting down on the time-consuming labor it can take to govern data, the following examples identify various data struggles that different organizations should be able to overcome by implementing their own data catalog(s). A data catalog offers a single place for data analysts to view and find all data assets across different departments. This consolidated view enables team members to share insights that can improve the business. For example, team members might discover cross-sell and upsell opportunities that can generate new revenue streams.

Seeking growth through customer-centric banking, an example company needed to reposition itself. The organization launched a plan that was predicted to increase revenue per customer by optimizing its cross-selling and upselling marketing campaigns. However, the bank always encountered the same roadblock: internal systems were not centered around their client relationships, making it nearly impossible to market to existing customers.

The organization had to create an analytical foundation, inclusive of a data catalog, to understand its customers' behaviors and needs on new levels of depth and granularity. It also used Cascading Style Sheets (CSS) to help standardize its business analytics reporting. The resulting comprehensive system and management solution delivered precisely targeted promotions to those customers deemed most likely to convert, helping increase outbound marketing campaign conversion rates by 10 percent.

Ungoverned sensitive data may lead to regulatory penalties. For instance, if an enterprise doing business in California does not rectify any of its violations against the California Consumer Privacy Act (CCPA), the state's attorney general could impose a civil penalty of $2,500 to $7,500 per violation. In Europe, when it comes to violations of the General Data Protection Regulation (GPDR), financial penalties could go as high as 20 million euros or 4 percent of a company's worldwide annual turnover. Therefore, as organizations face these and potentially growing data privacy regulations over the next few years, they must look more holistically at how they store and use data.

A data catalog can automate the classification and profiling of data assets and automatically enforce data protection rules established to anonymize and restrict access to sensitive information. More importantly, if something goes wrong, controls help the organization to respond to an issue more rapidly, whether that means flagging sensitive data, identifying and remediating issues, or collecting information in response to an audit. GDPR compliance requires companies that do business in Europe and possess personal data from EU data subjects are legally obligated to understand the types of data they store, where the data lives, and its associated levels of risk. (More information on this can be found at https://gdpr.eu.)

For a large organization operating in more than 150 countries, it can be a daunting task to refresh an organization's privacy practices and ensure that the GDPR guidelines are being met—all while enhancing products and services with a goal of ultimately benefiting its clients. To help enterprises successfully meet this task, IBM's Global Chief Data Office (GCDO) has created a global program to address the GDPR requirement and help clients more comprehensively understand the type of personal data the GDPR controls. The GCDO program is typically a service that Chief Data Officers within a global organization consult to set organizational data management policies.

The company in this example created a central data privacy catalog as a key first step in the journey to compliance, but it was still uncertain how to identify, evaluate, and share the discovered data that needed to be in compliance with the GDPR. As a result, the organization used its own existing cataloging technologies and created a central store for its privacy data. To complement the catalog, the organization also implemented a data risk-management application to provide a data risk-control center through which executives and its teams could view the updated information from the privacy catalog via a central dashboard to ensure that ongoing data privacy requirements were being met.

An integrated quality and governance platform helps manage data and protects it from misuse. For effective governance, an enterprise data catalog must be in place. Organizations can't effectively apply governance if they don't have organized data with proper metadata tags and lineage information. Data organization includes detailing each data object: documenting data properties, ownership, business context, origin, and structure; evaluating data quality; and consistently classifying data so it can automatically be used to define and refine an organization's DataOps practice.

When implementing various new systems and processes into their business, another organization found that governance in its enterprise was not a simple feat. The quantity of data it needed to keep track of was quickly multiplying, and it was losing track of where the data was located and how it could effectively use the data to benefit its business. By adopting an integrated approach that collected, defined, and managed its data all in one platform, the organization was able to cut 50 percent of its business systems, reduce its complex management of systems and data, and cut operational costs in order to maximize the organization's growth benefits. The company implemented a data cataloging technology that created consistent definitions of its business data and helped it better understand what its data could do.

In addition to the customer examples above, a data catalog can also help support a governed data lake and help enable AI governance. Data lake governance requires discipline, good policy, and collaboration between the people who manage data access and the people who access the data. Cataloging helps to tag the data in the data lake and create an inventory of information assets. The catalog interface provides data lake users with information about the data within its classification and lineage and how it's governed. The catalog can serve multiple stakeholders in the organization, eliminating inefficiencies associated with "lost in translation" issues.

A data catalog can help an enterprise governance program grow to support the maturing demands of AI. As AI takes root, businesses need an organizational approach toward developing policies that lets them create a framework to effectively design, deploy, and monitor AI-powered models and algorithms with a focus on fairness, accountability, transparency, safety, and privacy, to ensure unbiased and transparent outcomes. AI can help remove human bias by removing the emotion or prejudice from human decision-making.

Data Virtualization

Data virtualization is the other cornerstone of a data fabric architecture. Data is everywhere, and some of the best businesses in the world today are data-driven. Businesses are collecting data from more and increasingly diverse sources to analyze and run their operations, with those sources perhaps numbering in the thousands or millions, especially when considering embedded devices and the Internet of Things (IOT). The complexity, cost, time, and risk of error in collecting, governing, storing, processing, and analyzing that data centrally is increasing exponentially. In parallel, the databases and repositories that are the sources of this data are more powerful, with abundant processing and data storage capability of their own available and at hand.

Data virtualization helps connect many data sources into a single collection of data sources or databases, often referred to as a "constellation" (see Figure 8.1). Data virtualization removes the need to perform analytics queries on data copied and stored in a centralized location. The analytics application can submit a query that's processed on the server where the data source exists. Results of the query are consolidated within the constellation and returned to the original application. This means data continues to exist at the source and no data copying is necessary.

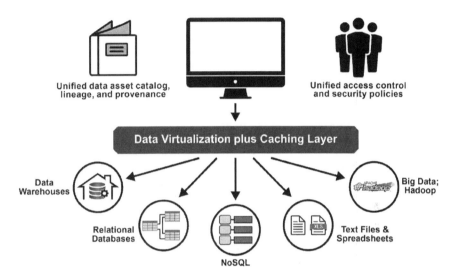

Figure 8.1: Example of data virtualization

Applications connect to a data virtualization service as if they are connecting to a single database. When connected, applications can submit queries against the system as if they were querying a single database. The workload is collaboratively distributed and computed by all participating data sources that have data relevant to the query. There are several important features that let data virtualization help businesses work more effectively with their data. Facilitating collaborative computing is one of them.

Using the processing power of every data source and accessing the data physically stored in each data source prevents the latency involved with moving and copying data. In addition, all repository data is accessible in real-time, and governance and erroneous-data issues are virtually eliminated. There's no need for ETL and duplicate data storage, which accelerates processing times. This results in bringing real-time insights to decision-making applications or analysts more quickly and dependably than existing methods. It also remains highly complementary with existing methods and can coexist when it remains necessary to copy and move some data for historical, archival, or regulatory purposes.

A typical scenario in distributed data systems is that many databases store data in a common schema. For example, an enterprise may have multiple databases storing sales data or transactional data, each for a set of tenants or a region. Data virtualization should automatically detect common schemas across systems and present them as a single schema, a process known as "schema folding." For example, a sales table that exists in each of 20 databases should be able to appear as a single sales table and let users query it via Structured Query Language (SQL) as one virtual table. Similarly, the right inline tools should make it possible to define table views across databases of different types and perhaps geographic locations, as shown in Figure 8.2.

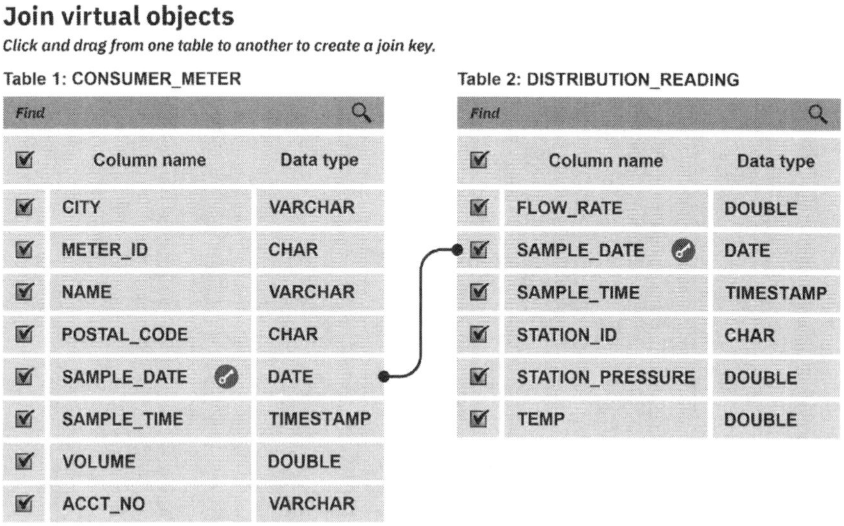

Join virtual objects

Click and drag from one table to another to create a join key.

Table 1: CONSUMER_METER

☑	Find	🔍
☑	Column name	Data type
☑	CITY	VARCHAR
☑	METER_ID	CHAR
☑	NAME	VARCHAR
☑	POSTAL_CODE	CHAR
☑	SAMPLE_DATE 🔗	DATE
☑	SAMPLE_TIME	TIMESTAMP
☑	VOLUME	DOUBLE
☑	ACCT_NO	VARCHAR

Table 2: DISTRIBUTION_READING

☑	Find	🔍
☑	Column name	Data type
☑	FLOW_RATE	DOUBLE
☑	SAMPLE_DATE 🔗	DATE
☑	SAMPLE_TIME	TIMESTAMP
☑	STATION_ID	CHAR
☑	STATION_PRESSURE	DOUBLE
☑	TEMP	DOUBLE

Figure 8.2: Intuitive interfaces make it simple to join table views

All communication within the constellation needs to be encrypted with security-rich, robust, and powerful technology, such as Secure Sockets Layer (SSL) and Transport Layer Security (TLS) encryption using standard protocols.

Data virtualization's design and architecture of, for example, a peer-to-peer computational mesh can provide a significant advantage over traditional federation architecture ("federation" is a pattern in enterprise architecture that allows interoperability and information-sharing between semi-autonomous, de-centrally organized lines of business (LOBs), information technology systems, and applications). A data virtualization engine can help rapidly deliver query results from multiple data sources by leveraging advanced parallel processing and optimizations. Collaborative, highly paralleled compute models can provide superior query performance compared to federation. Not only can data virtualization be fast, it can also automatically find databases and tables, making information queries from multiple data sources simpler. Queries should be able to span data and combine the results from multiple sources, including relational databases, NoSQL sources, spreadsheets, flat files, and other data stores.

Data sources appear to an application as a single instance of a database when using data virtualization. The technology should be able to convert to and from all the SQL dialects. Therefore, applications can freely code SQL, procedural language/SQL (PL/SQL), and SQL PL as if they are working directly on the source database without trying to determine whether the syntax is supported by the target data system. Popular languages should be able to leverage data virtualization without any modification or upgrade. Data virtualization is also well-suited to perform analytics on highly distributed data sets dispersed across many sources, particularly in cases where the data and the analytics results are time-sensitive. Effective where the analytics may be a one-time operation on that specific set of data, it's also applicable to scenarios where the latency for batch copying from some data sources exceeds the business need or service-level agreements for analytics results.

Another benefit of data virtualization is that it renders obsolete processes under which many organizations duplicate data and create new data repositories to satisfy the needs of specific lines of business for analytics. This process requires configuring physical assets and creating and maintaining new ETLs to load and transform the data to those repositories. Often the data is out of date by the time it becomes available to the line of business, and the process is also expensive.

Existing approaches are reaching the saturation point for many IT organizations. With the number and diversity of data sources and the need for analytics increasing, many existing methods are no longer scalable. Data virtualization can help increase the productivity of IT organizations and provide a scalable approach for individual lines of business to access enterprise-wide data.

In many instances, there are policy or legal issues with copying or moving data, such as personal information. These restrictions can get in the way of a business need for demographic analytics results. Data virtualization should help resolve these issues by leaving the protected data at the source and returning only the demographic query result. The privacy policies set by the administrator are enforced during the virtualization process, ensuring security for sensitive data.

A data scientist might need to create a data lake, copy data from the sources of interest, and integrate that data before being able to test out hypotheses with analytics. Data virtualization can help reduce the need for the data lake, enabling data scientists to access the data they require to test hypotheses by connecting directly to the data sources via their tools of choice.

In addition, data virtualization can help users acquire actionable, unified data when they want, in the way they want, at the speed matching their analytical needs. This technology leads to faster integration speed and performance, and improved decision-making that helps enterprises adapt more quickly to changing business demands. Data virtualization can support a range of key initiatives, including modernization for faster delivery of modern systems of engagement, real-time analytics that meet immediate business needs, and optimization that can reduce the cost and complexity of accessing organizational data.

Self-service BI can also be enabled using data virtualization. The virtual, reusable data assets provide a business-friendly representation of data, enabling the user to interact with data without having to know the complexities of the physical data layer or where the data is stored. It also lets multiple BI and reporting tools acquire data from a data virtualization layer.

Data virtualization should provide a unified 360-degree view. The virtualized data asset delivers a complete view of data in real-time. The virtual data layer serves as a unified, integrated view of business information that improves a user's ability to understand and use organizational data. Data virtualization should also provide agile service-oriented architecture (SOA) data services. A data virtualization layer delivers the data services layer to SOA applications. It speeds the creation of virtual assets (new assets, sometimes transient, that are often created from physical assets) without the need to touch underlying sources by using auto-discovery and mapping of metadata that encapsulates the data access logic. Data virtualization also lets multiple business services acquire data from a centralized location and provides loose coupling between business services and physical data sources.

Finally, data virtualization can provide improved control of information. It improves data quality through centralized access control and provides a robust security infrastructure and reduction in physical copies of data, thus decreasing risk. The metadata repository catalogs an organization's data stores and the relationships between the data in various data stores, enabling transparency and visibility across data relationships and lineage. Data virtualization can be the solution for overcoming the shortcomings of a centralized repository.

Data Virtualization vs. Data Federation

It's important to understand the difference between data virtualization and data federation. Data federation is the technology that lets an organization logically map remote data sources and execute distributed queries against those multiple sources from a single location. Data virtualization, on the other hand, is a platform that provides the end-user experience, enabling users to retrieve and manipulate data without requiring them to know any technical details about the data (how it is formatted or where it is physically located). Data virtualization provides the end user a self-service data mart of multiple data sources that can be joined into a single customer view.

The importance of modernizing an organization's underlying data management can't be overstated. By leveraging data virtualization, ML-powered SQL queries, and containerization, enterprises can make data more accessible across the whole organization. This can result in lower operational costs, faster query performance, improved analytics, highly secured data, and more agile development.

9

How IBM Delivers Value Through the Data Fabric

IBM delivers data fabric capabilities as part of the IBM Cloud Pak for Data product previously described. To provide examples of how this can aid an enterprise, it's useful to walk through some of the key steps of using Cloud Pak for Data to implement four use cases:

- Data governance and privacy

- Customer-360

- MLOps and trustworthy AI

- Multicloud data integration

The use cases are based on a fictional company named "Golden Bank." Any similarity to other organizations with the same or similar name are completely coincidental. Each use case describes:

- The technologies an organization should use at each stage

- The actions that should be taken at each stage

- The value the technologies deliver

When implementing the data fabric solution on Cloud Pak for Data, organizations can address the challenges of data access, data quality, data governance, and management of their data and AI lifecycles.

The data fabric solution on Cloud Pak for Data provides capabilities for managing and automating data and AI lifecycles, including these:

- Data access: The ability to access data across multiple clouds and on-premises in an existing data architecture

- Self-service consumption: The ability to share and use data and other assets from across the enterprise in catalogs

- Accumulated knowledge: The ability to understand data through a common business vocabulary and to trust the data through history, lineage, and quality analysis

- Collaborative innovation: The ability to collaborate with others to discover insights, which includes preparing data, analyzing data, and building models with a set of integrated tools for all levels of experience

- Data governance, security, and compliance: The ability to automatically enforce uniform data privacy across the platform

- Unified lifecycle: The ability to automate the building, testing, deploying, and monitoring of data pipelines and AI models

With a data fabric, an organization can help transform data into assets that accumulate meaning and value. This means assets are more than just data. When first creating a connection to a data source, a user may have basic information about how to access data, tables, schemas, and data values. Users may start adding value while ingesting data by virtualizing, transforming, or replicating it in workspaces called "projects."

When users curate data, they add metadata to the data assets. Users profile the data to classify it and compile statistics about its values. They enrich assets with business terms that describe the semantic meaning of the data for an organization. They analyze data quality. When a user publishes the assets into a catalog to share them with the wider organization, the assets are automatically protected by the rules that were created to control who can access which data.

As authorized users find data assets in catalogs and use the assets in projects, they create the "third level of meaning" that describes the history of how the asset is used, the lineage of the data, and the relationships between assets. Users can synthesize data into a 360-degree view of customers, analyze the data in notebooks or dashboards, or train ML models.

Figure 9.1 shows how data assets increase in value through the data fabric.

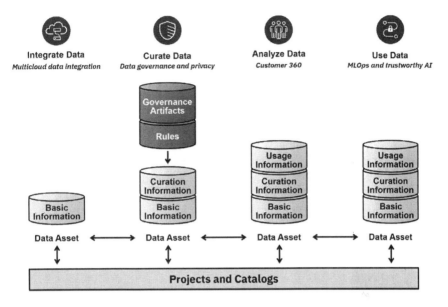

Figure 9.1: Assets can increase in value through the data fabric

Models are also assets. Users can track deployments and input data for the model, comparisons between models, and compliance with corporate protocols.

Cloud Pak for Data provides four use cases mentioned at the start of this chapter as parts of the data fabric solution as shown in Figure 9.2. An organization can implement a data fabric as represented in each use case by installing one or more services that provide features and tools. Some services are included in multiple use cases.

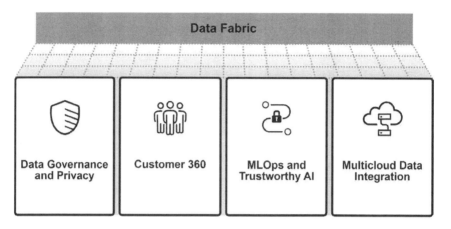

Figure 9.2: IBM data fabric use cases

Use cases represent ways to implement part of a data fabric solution so that teams can start working while other teams build out other parts. An organization can start with any use case and add the others as needed. For example:

- If a user has a more-mature governance model, start by building a governance foundation, as described in the data governance and privacy use case.

- If a user wants quicker time-to-value, start with data virtualization or data science, as described in the multicloud data integration and the MLOps and trustworthy AI use cases.

- If a user is focused on a customer-centric transformation, start consolidating customer data, as described in the customer-360 use case.

Use case #1 (below) is a data governance and privacy scenario, in which it's important to implement governance based on metadata that provides business knowledge and defines data protection. Also key is providing high-quality data assets in self-service catalogs and automating enforcement of data governance for regulatory compliance. (Service for this data governance and privacy scenario: Watson Knowledge Catalog)

In a customer-360 generic scenario, which makes up use case #2, central to success is creating a comprehensive view of enterprise customers that is augmented by AI-driven insights to enable smarter customer interactions. (Services for this customer-360 scenario: IBM Match 360 with Watson and Watson Knowledge Catalog)

In the MLOps and trustworthy AI example, use case #3, the central activities are building and operationalizing AI with an automated and governed workflow that enforces fairness, quality, and explainability in a data model. (Services for this use case: Watson Studio, Watson Machine Learning, and Watson Knowledge Catalog)

In the multicloud data integration use case (#4), key actions are simplifying and automating access to all enterprise data without moving it and orchestrating data across a distributed landscape to create a network of instantly available information for data consumers. (Services for this use case: Data Virtualization, DataStage, and Watson Knowledge Catalog)

Use Case 1: Data Governance and Privacy

Data governance and privacy are key challenges for enterprises that need to balance the benefits of providing access to data with protecting sensitive data. Cloud Pak for Data provides the methods an enterprise can use to automate data governance and privacy to ensure data accessibility, trust, protection, security, and compliance.

Many enterprises face the following data governance and privacy challenges:

- Providing data privacy at scale: The organization must comply with data privacy regulations for data in data sources across multiple cloud platforms and on-premises.

- Accessing high-quality data: The organization must provide access to high-quality enterprise data across multiple teams.

- Providing self-service data consumption: The organization must ensure that data consumers, such as data scientists, don't struggle to find and use the data that they need.

These challenges can be met by implementing a data fabric with Cloud Pak for Data, as shown in this example of Golden Bank's challenges. Golden Bank has a large amount of customer and mortgage data that includes sensitive information. The bank wants to ensure the quality of the data, mask the sensitive information, and make it available for use across several departments. To implement data governance and privacy, Golden Bank followed this process:

1. Set up a governance framework.

2. Create rules to protect data.

3. Curate data to share in catalogs.

4. Find and use data.

The Watson Knowledge Catalog service in Cloud Pak for Data provides the tools and processes that Golden Bank needs to implement a data governance and privacy solution, as shown in Figure 9.3.

Data governance and privacy use case

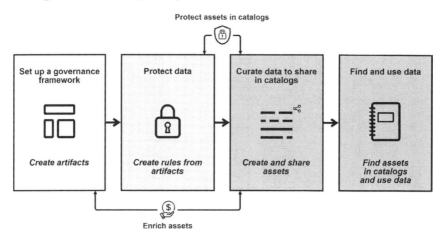

Figure 9.3: Tools and processes organizations need in order to implement a data governance and privacy solution

Let's explore each of these steps in more detail.

Step 1: Set up a governance framework.

To meet all three of the challenges, Golden Bank's team needs to set up a framework of governance artifacts that act as metadata to classify and describe the data:

- Before the team can automate data privacy, it needs to ensure that the data to control is accurately identified.

- Before the team can analyze data quality, it needs to identify the format of the data.

- To make data easy to find, the team needs to ensure that the content of the data is accurately described.

In this first step of the process, Golden Bank's governance team can build on the foundation of the predefined governance artifacts and create custom governance artifacts that are specific to its organization. It can create artifacts to describe the format, business meaning, sensitivity, range of values, and governance policies of the data.

What to Use	How to Use It	Best to Use When
Categories	Use the predefined category to store governance artifacts. Create categories to organize governance artifacts in a hierarchical structure similar to folders. Add collaborators with roles that define their permissions on the artifacts in the category.	Users need more than the predefined category. Organization needs more fine-grained control of who can own, author, and view governance artifacts.
Workflows	Use the default workflow configuration that does not restrict who creates governance artifacts or require reviews. Configure workflows for governance artifacts and designate who can create which types of governance artifacts in which categories.	Organization needs to control who creates governance artifacts. Organization needs prepublication review of draft governance artifacts.
Governance Artifacts	Use the predefined data classes and classifications. Create governance artifacts that act as metadata to enrich, define, and control data assets.	Organization needs to add knowledge and meaning to assets to help people understand the data. Organization needs to improve data quality analysis.
Knowledge Accelerators	Import a set of predefined governance artifacts to improve data classification, regulatory compliance, self-service analytics, and other governance operations.	Organization needs a standard vocabulary to describe business issues, business performance, industry standards, and regulations. Organization needs to save time by importing precreated governance artifacts.

The governance team leader at Golden Bank starts by creating a category, **Banking**, to hold the governance artifacts that the team plans to create. The team leader adds the rest of the governance team members as collaborators to the Banking category, including the **Editor** role so that Editor team members have permission to create governance artifacts. Then, the team leader configures workflows so that a different team member is responsible for creating each type of artifact. All workflows require an approval step by the team leader. One governance team member imports a set of business terms from a spreadsheet. Some of the business terms differentiate between personal and commercial clients. Another team member creates a reference data set, "Diamond-level client names," which contains a list of the top commercial clients. A third team member creates a custom data class, "Diamond-level clients," to identify the top commercial clients, based on the reference data set.

Step 2: Create rules to protect data.

In the next step of the process, the team sets up rules to ensure compliance with data privacy regulations by controlling who can see what data. The team creates data protection rules that protect data across the platform. The team can then use these rules to mask sensitive data based on the content, format, or meaning of the data, or the identity of the users who access the data.

What to Use	How to Use It	Best to Use When
Data Protection Rules	Protect sensitive information from unauthorized access by denying access or masking data values in data assets. Dynamically and consistently mask data at a user-defined granular level.	Organization needs to automatically enforce data privacy across the platform. Organization needs to retain availability and utility of data while also complying with privacy regulations.
Masking Flows	Use advanced format-preserving data-masking capabilities when extracting copies or subsets of production data.	Organization needs anonymized training data and test sets that retain data integrity.
Policies and Governance Rules	Describe and document the organization's guidelines, regulations, standards, or procedures for data security. Describe the required behavior or actions to implement the governance policy.	The organization needs the people who use the data understand the data governance policies.

To create a predictive model for mortgage approvals, Golden Bank's data scientists need access to data sets that include sensitive data. For

example, the data scientists want to access the table with data about
mortgage applicants, which includes a column with Social Security
Numbers. A governance team member creates a data-protection rule that
masks Social Security Numbers. If the assigned data class of a column in
a data asset is "US Social Security Number," the values in that column
are replaced with 10 *Xs*. Another governance team member creates a
policy that includes the data-protection rule. The policy describes the
business reasons for implementing the rule. Later, when users, such as
data scientists, see the masked icon on a data column, they can view the
data-protection rule, and then view the associated policy to understand
why the data is masked.

Step 3: Curate data to share in catalogs.

Data stewards curate high-quality data assets in "projects" and publish
them to catalogs where the people who need the data can find them.
Data stewards enrich the data assets by assigning governance artifacts as
metadata that describes the data and informs the semantic search for data.

What to Use	How to Use It	Best to Use When
Metadata Import	Automatically import technical metadata for the data that is associated with a connection to create data assets.	Organization needs to create many data assets from a data source. Organization needs to refresh previously imported data assets.
Metadata Enrichment	Profile multiple data assets in a single run to automatically assign data classes and identify data types and formats of columns. Automatically assign business terms to assets and generate term suggestions based on data classification. Rerun the import and the enrichment jobs at intervals to discover and evaluate changes to data assets.	Organization needs to curate and publish many imported data assets.
Data Quality Analysis	Run quality analysis on multiple data sets in a single run to scan for common dimensions of data quality, such as missing values or data class violations. Continuously track changes to content and structure of data, and recurringly analyze changed data.	Organization needs to know whether the quality of its data might affect the accuracy of its data analysis or models. Users need ability to identify which data sets to remediate.
Catalogs	Publish curated assets to share among the organizational collaborators.	Organization needs a central repository to store data assets that displays the associated metadata, relationships, and history of the assets.

The data stewards on the governance team start importing metadata to create data assets in a project. After metadata import, Golden Bank has two data assets that represent tables with a column that is named "ID." After metadata enrichment, those columns are clearly differentiated by their assigned metadata:

- One column is assigned the business terms "Commercial client" and "Company identifier" and the data class "Diamond-level clients."

- The other column is assigned the business terms "Personal identifier" and "Private individual" and the data class "US Social Security Number."

The data stewards run data-quality analysis on the data assets to make sure that the overall data-quality score exceeds the Golden Bank threshold of 95 percent. The governance team leader creates a catalog called "Mortgage Approval Catalog" and adds the data stewards and data scientists as catalog collaborators. The data stewards publish the data assets that they created in the project into the catalog.

Step 4: Find and use data.

The catalog helps Golden Bank's teams understand the data and makes the right data available for the right use. Data scientists and other types of users can help themselves to the data that they need while they remain compliant with corporate access and data-protection policies. They can add data assets from a catalog into a project, where they collaborate to prepare, analyze, and model the data.

What to Use	How to Use It	Best to Use When
Catalogs	Organize assets to share among the organizational collaborators. Take advantage of AI-powered semantic search and recommendations to help users find what they need.	Users need to more easily understand, collaborate on, enrich, and access the high-quality data. Organization needs to increase visibility of data and collaboration between business users. Organization needs users to view, access, manipulate, and analyze data without understanding its physical format or location, and without having to move or copy it. Organization needs users to be able to enhance assets by rating and reviewing assets.

What to Use	How to Use It	Best to Use When
Global Search	Search for assets across all the projects, catalogs, and deployment spaces to which users have access. Search for governance artifacts across the categories to which users have access.	Users need to find data, another type of asset, or a governance artifact.
Data Refinery	Cleanse data to fix or remove data that is incorrect, incomplete, improperly formatted, or duplicated. Shape data to customize it by filtering, sorting, combining, or removing columns.	Organization needs to improve the quality or usefulness of data.

The data scientists find the data assets that they need in the catalog and copy those assets to a project. In their project, the data scientists can refine the data to prepare it for training a model.

Use Case 2: Customer-360

If an enterprise needs to ensure that its users and systems have a total, trusted, unified view of the customer data, Cloud Pak for Data provides the platform and tools to create a comprehensive view of customers by connecting data across domains and presenting that data in interactive dashboards. Golden Bank needs to provide a trusted and unified view of customer data to tackle these challenges:

- Connecting key sources of customer data: Rather than repeatedly collecting data, Golden Bank needs to connect to key sources of customer data at the time of analysis.

- Breaking down silos: The organization needs to bring together disparate data into a single, 360-degree, integrated view of its customers. (While there is a technical component to achieving this, there are often cultural and political barriers that also need to be addressed.)

- Creating a complete customer profile: The team needs to build accurate views of customers at scale, quickly, to optimize self-service processes and data stewardship.

- Making data available for users: Data engineers need to be able to publish the customer data to a single catalog where all users who need to consume the data have self-service access to it.

Golden Bank wants to run a campaign to offer lower mortgage rates. The bank needs a 360-degree view of customer data combined with credit-score data to see the complete picture before offering mortgages to customers. To implement a customer-360 use case, Golden Bank followed this process:

1. Configure a 360-degree view of its customers

2. Explore a 360-degree view of its customers

3. Share the data

The IBM Match 360 and Watson Knowledge Catalog services in Cloud Pak for Data provide all of the tools and processes that Golden Bank organization needs to implement a customer-360 solution as shown in Figure 9.4.

Customer 360 use case

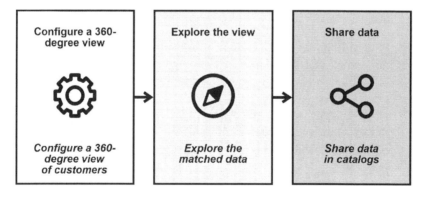

Figure 9.4: Tools and processes organizations need in order to implement a customer-360 solution

Let's break down these process steps.

Step 1: Configure a 360-degree view of the customers.

In this first step of the process, data engineers can configure a 360-degree view of Golden Bank's customers by combining data from disparate sources, generating and refining a data model, and mapping the data into the data model.

What to Use	How to Use It	Best to Use When
Configuration Tools	With the configuration tools in IBM Match 360, data engineers can gather customer data from different systems across the enterprise and view an automatically generated, customizable data model without manually mapping thousands of attributes. After loading the data into IBM Match 360, data engineers can run a matching algorithm to create enriched master data entities.	Organization needs to use an intelligent matching algorithm that personnel can tune and train to establish a single, trusted, 360-degree view of data.

Data engineers at Golden Bank combine customer data from various sources with credit-score data to resolve entities across the data and create a consolidated 360-degree view of the customers. The engineers set up and add assets to the master data, map the data asset attributes, publish the data model, and run the matching algorithm to prepare the data to be explored.

Step 2: Explore a 360-degree view of the customers.

Data analysts and other business users explore the matched data.

What to Use	How to Use It	Best to Use When
Master Data Explorer	With the master data explorer in IBM Match 360, users and systems search, view, and analyze master data entities. Users can discover master data directly in the space where they expect to consume it.	Users and systems need a total view of the data. Users and systems need to search, view, and analyze master data entities. Organization needs to use APIs to connect its business applications to trusted master data.

Golden Bank data engineers have configured a 360-degree view of customers by combining customer data with credit-score data. After this, data analysts analyze, explore, and validate the results in IBM Match 360 to identify and select the best qualifying customers to target for marketing campaign offers.

Step 3: Share the data.

The catalog helps Golden Bank's teams understand the customer data and makes the right data available for the right use. Data scientists and other types of users can help themselves to the matched and published customer data that they need while they remain compliant with corporate access and data protection policies. They can add data assets from a catalog into a project, where they collaborate to prepare, analyze, and model the data.

What to Use	How to Use It	Best to Use When
Watson Knowledge Catalog: Catalogs	Organize data assets to share among organizational collaborators. Take advantage of AI-powered semantic search and recommendations to help users find what they need.	Users need to easily understand, collaborate on, enrich, and access the high-quality data. Organization needs to increase visibility of data and collaboration between business users. Users need to view, access, manipulate, and analyze data without understanding its physical format or location, and without having to move or copy it. Users need to enhance assets by rating and reviewing assets.

The data stewards find the matched customer data assets that they need in the catalog and copy those assets to a project. In their project, the data scientists can refine the data to prepare it for training a model.

Use Case 3: MLOps and Trustworthy AI

To manage data and model assets across the AI lifecycle, an enterprise needs integrated systems and processes. Cloud Pak for Data provides the processes and technologies to enable an enterprise to develop, deploy, maintain, and manage ML and AI models in production. The challenges are establishing an MLOps and trustworthy AI solution for the enterprise, which involves tackling these challenges:

- Managing the full AI lifecycle: The organization needs to manage the full AI lifecycle from a single platform with integrated services that support the building and training of all models and the monitoring of those models in production.

- Streamlining model development, model validation, and model deployment: The organization needs to operate trusted AI through ongoing model monitoring and retraining on an end-to-end unified data and AI platform and then use the resulting predictions to inform actions to address user needs.

- Ensuring trust in models, processes, and data: The organization needs to provide private data within models that are fair and explainable, and that includes automated processes that ensure consistency, efficiency, and transparency at scale.

An MLOps automated lifecycle with data fabric on Cloud Pak for Data can help solve these challenges.

Data scientists at Golden Bank need to create a mortgage-approval model that avoids unanticipated risk and treats all applicants fairly by creating an MLOps and trustworthy AI process to expand its business by offering low-rate mortgage renewals for online applications.

To implement MLOps and trustworthy AI for their enterprise, Golden Bank data scientists follow this process:

1. Share the data

2. Build and train models

3. Deploy models

4. Monitor models

5. Track models

6. Automate the AI lifecycle

The Watson Studio, Watson Machine Learning, and Watson Knowledge Catalog services in Cloud Pak for Data provide the tools and processes that an organization needs to implement a MLOps and trustworthy AI solution as shown in Figure 9.5.

MLOps and trustworthy AI use case

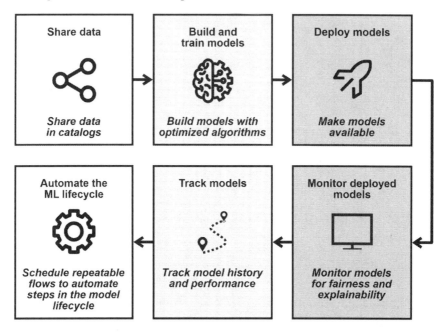

Figure 9.5: Tools and processes that organizations need in order to implement a MLOps and trustworthy AI solution

Steps in the process include several activities.

Step 1: Share the data.

The catalog helps Golden Bank teams understand their customer data and makes the right data available for the right use. Data scientists and other types of users can help themselves to the data that they need while they remain compliant with corporate access and data-protection policies. They can add data assets from a catalog into a project, where they collaborate to prepare, analyze, and model the data.

What to Use	How to Use It	Best to Use When
Catalogs	Use catalogs in Watson Knowledge Catalog to organize data assets to share among organizational collaborators. Take advantage of AI-powered semantic search and recommendations to help users find what they need.	Users need to more easily understand, collaborate on, enrich, and access the high-quality data. Organization needs to increase visibility of data and collaboration between business users. Users need to view, access, manipulate, and analyze data without understanding its physical format or location, and without having to move or copy it. Organization needs users to enhance assets by rating and reviewing them.

Golden Bank's governance team leader creates a catalog, "Mortgage Approval Catalog," and adds the data stewards and data scientists as catalog collaborators. The data stewards publish the data assets that they created into the catalog. The data scientists find the data assets, curated by the data stewards, in the catalog and copy those assets to a project. In their project, the data scientists can refine the data to prepare it for training a model.

Step 2: Build and train models.

To get predictive insights based on their data, data scientists, business analysts, and ML engineers can build and train models. Data scientists use Cloud Pak for Data services to build the AI models, ensuring that the right algorithms and optimizations are being used to make predictions that help to solve business problems.

What to Use	How to Use It	Best to Use When
AutoAI	Use AutoAI in Watson Studio to automatically select algorithms, engineer features, generate pipeline candidates, and train model pipeline candidates. Then, evaluate the ranked pipelines and save the best as models. Deploy the trained models to a space or export the model training pipeline that provides the most value from AutoAI into a notebook to refine it.	Organization needs an advanced and automated way to build a good set of training pipelines and models quickly. Organization needs to be able to export the generated pipelines to refine them.

What to Use	How to Use It	Best to Use When
Notebooks and Scripts	Use notebooks and scripts in Watson Studio to write new feature-engineering, model training, and evaluation code in Python or R, based on training data sets that are available in the project, or connections to data sources such as databases, data lakes, or object storage. Use the organization's approved algorithms and libraries.	Organization needs to use Python or R coding skills to have full control over the code that creates, trains, and evaluates the models.
SPSS Modeler Flows	Use SPSS Modeler flows in Watson Studio to create model training, evaluation, and scoring flows based on training data sets that are available in the project, or connections to data sources such as databases, data lakes, or object storage.	Organization needs a simple way to explore data and define model training, evaluation, and scoring flows.
RStudio Server with R 3.6	Analyze data and build and test models by working with R in an RStudio Server with R 3.6 development environment.	Organization needs to use a development environment to work in R.
Watson Machine Learning Accelerator	Train neural networks by using a deep-learning experiment builder.	Organization needs to train thousands of models, train deeper neural networks, and explore more complicated hyperparameter spaces.
Decision Optimization	Prepare data, import models, solve problems, compare scenarios, visualize data, find solutions, produce reports, and save models to deploy with Watson Machine Learning.	Organization needs to evaluate millions of possibilities to find the best solution to a prescriptive analytics problem.

Data scientists at Golden Bank create a model, "Mortgage Approval Model" that avoids unanticipated risk and treats all applicants fairly. They add the model entry to the "Mortgage Approval Catalog" and then run a notebook to build the model and automatically capture metadata that can be used later to track the model using factsheets. The data scientists train the model to predict which applicants qualify for mortgages.

Step 3: Deploy models.

When operations team members deploy their AI models, the models become available for applications to use for scoring and predictions to help drive actions.

What to Use	How to Use It	Best to Use When
Spaces User Interface (UI)	Use the Spaces UI in Watson Machine Learning to deploy models and other assets from projects to spaces.	When users prefer a UI.
Command-Line Tool (cpdctl)	Use the cpdctl command-line tool in Watson Machine Learning to manage the lifecycle of models, including the configuration settings, and to automate an end-to-end flow that includes training the model, saving it, creating a deployment space, and deploying the model.	Organization needs to deploy and manage models to test or production environments from a command-line.

The operations team members at Golden Bank promote the "Mortgage Approval Model" from the project to a deployment space to create an online model deployment.

Step 4: Monitor deployed models.

After deploying models, it's important to govern and monitor them to make sure that they are explainable and transparent. Data scientists need to be able to explain how the models arrive at certain predictions so that they can determine whether the predictions have any implicit or explicit bias. In addition, it's a best practice to watch for model performance and data consistency issues during the lifecycle of the model.

What to Use	How to Use It	Best to Use When
Watson OpenScale	Monitor model fairness issues across multiple features. Monitor model performance and data consistency over time. Explain how the model arrived at certain predictions with weight factors. Maintain and report on model governance and lifecycle across the organization.	The data contains features that are protected or that might contribute to prediction fairness. Organization needs to trace model performance and data consistencies over time. Organization needs to know why the model gives certain predictions.

Data scientists at Golden Bank use Watson Studio to monitor the deployed "Mortgage Approval Model" to ensure that it is accurate and is treating all Golden Bank mortgage applicants fairly. They run a notebook to set up monitors for the model and then tweak the configuration by using the Watson OpenScale user interface. Using metrics from the Watson Studio quality monitor and fairness monitor, the data scientists determine how well the model predicts outcomes and whether it produces any biased outcomes. They also gain an understanding of how the model comes to decisions so that the decisions can be explained to the mortgage applicants.

Step 5: Track models.

In addition to monitoring data models for fairness and explainability, the organization needs to track the production models to ensure that they are performing well.

What to Use	How to Use It	Best to Use When
Factsheets	In the model inventory in a catalog in Watson Knowledge Catalog, view lifecycle status for all the registered assets and drill down to detailed factsheets for models or deployments registered to the model entry. View general model details, training information and metrics, and input and output schema. View general deployment details, evaluation details, quality metrics, fairness details, and drift details.	Organization needs to make sure that a model is performing as expected. Organization needs to determine whether adjustments are required.

Business analysts at Golden Bank request a "Mortgage Approval Model." They can then track the model through all stages of the AI lifecycle as data scientists build and train the model and ModelOps engineers deploy and evaluate it. Factsheets document details about the model history and generate metrics that show its performance.

Enterprise teams can automate and simplify the MLOps and AI lifecycle with Watson Studio pipelines.

What to Use	How to Use It	Best to Use When
Pipelines	Use pipelines in Watson Studio to create repeatable and scheduled flows that automate notebook, Data Refinery, and machine-learning pipelines, from data ingestion to model training, testing, and deployment.	Organization needs to automate any or all of the steps in the MLOps flow.

The data scientists at Golden Bank can also use pipelines to automate their complete MLOps and trustworthy AI lifecycle and processes to simplify the mortgage-approval process.

Step 6: Automate the ML lifecycle.

A team can automate and simplify the MLOps and AI lifecycle with Watson Studio pipelines.

What to Use	How to Use It	Best to Use When
Pipelines	Use pipelines in Watson Studio to create repeatable and scheduled flows that automate notebook, Data Refinery, and machine-learning pipelines, from data ingestion to model training, testing, and deployment.	Automate any or all of the steps in the MLOps flow.

Example: Golden Bank's Automated ML Lifecycle

The data scientists at Golden Bank can also use pipelines to automate their complete MLOps and trustworthy AI lifecycle and processes to simplify the mortgage-approval process.

Use Case 4: Multicloud Data Integration

To cope with the influx of data volumes and disparate data sources, enterprises need to build automation and intelligence into their data-integration processes. Cloud Pak for Data provides the platform and tools to orchestrate data dynamically and intelligently as applications need and consume it, using AI to predict how and when to leverage and automate tasks across a distributed landscape to create a high-performance network of readily available information for data consumers.

As their data types and volumes grow, enterprises face the following data integration challenges:

- Ingesting data from across the enterprise: An organization's processes need to be able to ingest data from any application or system, regardless of whether the data resides on-premises, in the cloud, or in a hybrid environment.

- Integrating data from multiple sources: The organization needs to be able to automate the bulk ingestion, cleansing, and complex transformations of data.

- Making data available for users: Data engineers need to be able to publish each integrated data set to a single catalog, and all users who need to consume the data need to have self-service access to it. Organizations can solve these challenges by implementing multicloud data integration with data fabric on Cloud Pak for Data.

Golden Bank has a large amount of customer and mortgage data that is stored in three external data sources. Lenders use this information to help them decide whether they should approve or deny mortgage applications. The bank wants to integrate the data from the different sources and then deliver that transformed data to a single output file that internal users can share.

To implement a multicloud data integration solution for its enterprise, Golden Bank organization follows this process:

1. Integrate the data

2. Share the data

The DataStage, Data Virtualization, and Watson Knowledge Catalog services in Cloud Pak for Data provide all of the tools and processes that Golden Bank needs to implement a multicloud data integration solution as shown in Figure 9.6.

Multicloud data integration use case

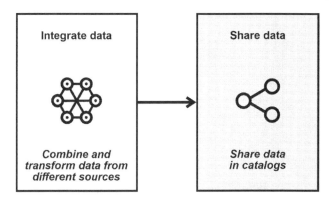

Figure 9.6: Tools and processes organizations need to implement a multicloud data integration solution

Step 1: Integrate the data.

With a data fabric architecture that uses Cloud Pak for Data, data engineers can optimize data integration by using workloads and data policies to efficiently access and work with data and combine virtualized data from different sources, types, and clouds as if the data were from a single data source. In this step of the process, the raw data is extracted, ingested, virtualized, and transformed into consumable, high-quality data that is ready to be explored and then orchestrated in the enterprise's AI lifecycle.

What to Use	How to Use It	Best to Use When
Data Virtualization	Query many data sources as one. Data engineers can create virtual data tables that can combine, join, or filter data from various relational data sources. Data engineers can then make the resulting combined live data available as data assets in Watson Knowledge Catalog. For example, they can use the combined live data to feed dashboards, notebooks, and flows to explore data.	Organization needs to combine live data from multiple sources to generate views and make combined data available as data assets in a catalog.
DataStage	Data engineers can design and run complex data flows that move and transform data.	Organization needs to design and run complex data flows that handle large volumes of data and connect to a wide range of data sources, integrate and transform data, and deliver it to target systems in batch or real-time.
Data Refinery	Access and refine data from diverse data-source connections. Materialize the resulting data sets as snapshots in time that might combine, join, filter, or mask data to make it usable for data scientists to analyze and explore. Make the resulting data sets available to the project in Watson Knowledge Catalog.	Users need to visualize the data when they want to make changes to it. Organization needs to simplify the process of preparing large amounts of raw data for analysis.

Risk analysts at Golden Bank calculate the daily interest rate that they recommend offering to borrowers for each credit-score range. Data engineers use DataStage to aggregate anonymized mortgage application data with the Personally Identifiable Information (PII) from mortgage applicants. DataStage integrates this information, including credit-score information for each applicant, the applicant's total debt, and an interest-rate lookup table. The data engineers then load the data into a target output .csv file that can be published to a catalog and shared for use by lenders and analysts.

Step 2: Share the data.

The catalog helps enterprise teams understand customer data and makes the right data available for the right use. Data scientists and other types of users can help themselves to the integrated data that they need while they remain compliant with corporate access and data-protection policies. They can add data assets from a catalog into a project, where they collaborate to prepare, analyze, and model the data.

What to Use	How to Do It	Best to Use When
Catalogs	Use catalogs in Watson Knowledge Catalog to organize data assets to share among the organizational collaborators. Take advantage of AI-powered semantic search and recommendations to help users find what they need.	Users need to understand, collaborate on, enrich, and access the high-quality data. Organization needs to increase visibility of data and collaboration between business users. Users need to view, access, manipulate, and analyze data without understanding its physical format or location, and without having to move or copy it. Organization needs users to enhance assets by rating and reviewing them.

The governance team leader at Golden Bank creates a catalog, "Mortgage Approval Catalog," and adds the data stewards and data scientists as catalog collaborators. The data stewards publish the data assets that they created into the catalog. The data scientists find the data assets, curated by the data stewards, in the catalog and copy those assets to a project. In their project, the data scientists can refine the data to prepare it for training a model.

A fifth data fabric use case focusing on data observability through the Databand.ai acquisition will be covered in an update to this book.

10

Conclusion

People and organizations have been collecting, organizing, and analyzing their data in the hope of trying to gain the deepest and most accurate insights to support and optimize their decision-making to achieve smarter business outcomes. Data continues to grow and proliferate across multiple spreadsheets, documents, multimedia sources, devices, databases, Hadoop stores, data marts, data warehouses, data lakes, and data lakehouses. There have been many attempts at representing and integrating disparate data sources that on their own fell short of expectations.

Although many organizations recognized that AI could be a competitive differentiator delivering agility and insights through trends that help predict what might happen next with recommended prescriptive actions, those same organization hit many implementation roadblocks.

It's been said many times that there can be no effective artificial intelligence (AI) without an effective Information Architecture (IA). What we have attempted to demonstrate is that the data fabric approach can provide a way through the enterprise jungle of data and applications found in many IT and information architectures, on which previous approaches and paradigms have fallen short of delivering.

Cloud technologies can help enable and provision assets as a set of location-independent and platform-agnostic services, effectively and efficiently, by delivering infrastructure, platform, data, software, security, and more "as a Service." Each of these can be more easily conceptualized as a set of containerized micro services that can be managed through a platform such as the Red Hat OpenShift Container Platform, as opposed to large monolithic applications that don't lend themselves to being recomposed or orchestrated. (See https://en.wikipedia.org/wiki/As_a_ service for more "as a Service" examples.)

While a hybrid cloud may provide more flexibility for an organization to place its data, applications, and processes where it makes most business sense, a hybrid cloud may also be viewed as a daunting concept by some. An organization needs to have the ability to seamlessly integrate and manage its assets across on-premises, private cloud, and public cloud infrastructures. Organizations need the flexibility to deploy and manage their assets locally, or as a service, within a fully or partially managed cloud infrastructure, depending on the needs of the organization and indeed each department.

It is to meet this need that IBM designed and delivers its data fabric capabilities as part of a unified, integrated, collaborative data and AI platform known as Cloud Pak for Data. The IBM Cloud Pak for Data platform offers a comprehensive set of capabilities, delivered as containerized services built on Red Hat OpenShift. This helps make the platform portable and scalable across the major industry (and other) hyperscalers and is available and consumable in a range of different form factors and deployment options designed to suit ever-changing business needs and budgets.

A data fabric is fundamental to the success of a data and AI platform, due in part to the data fabric's key concepts shown in Figure 10.1.

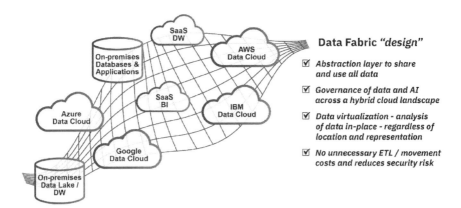

Figure 10.1: Concepts of a data fabric

A data fabric, if implemented as part of a data and AI enterprise–hardened platform can deliver the following benefits:

For technical teams and CTOs:

- Decreased effort to maintain data-quality standards due to fewer data versions

- Reduced infrastructure and storage costs (consolidated data-management tools and reduction in data copies)

- Faster and simplified data-delivery processes because there are fewer targets to reach and advanced optimization of data flows

- Reduction in efforts for data access management as it gets automated by global data policy enforcement.

For business teams and CDOs:

- Gaining faster and more-accurate insights due to easy access to high-quality data

- Ability to focus time on analyzing rather than finding and preparing data

- Streamlined full self-service data-shopping experience

- Avoidance of biased analysis due to data restrictions

- Increased compliance *and security* despite full analytics utilization

How to get started can be perceived as a challenge for many organizations. A methodology outline based on the authors' combined 60 years in the computing industry is as follows:

- Select one business problem that is keeping the CTO and/or CDO awake at night. The project chosen will need to have strong executive sponsorship from stakeholders that are personally invested in its success.

- Perform a readiness/maturity assessment to determine where the enterprise is in terms of its data and AI journey. (Find out more about assessing this journey to AI: https://ai-journey.mybluemix. net.)

- Engage industry analysts and their reports to determine which vendors are the leaders when it comes to completeness of vision and ability to execute.

- Sign up for trials of solutions to experience how well a product delivers against the specific needs of the enterprise's environment. (Find out more about the IBM Cloud Pak for Data as a Service free trial: https://dataplatform.cloud.ibm.com/registration/stepone?apps =all&context=cpdaas.)

- Engage expertise from services and consulting organizations that offer proven agile methodologies that can deliver and demonstrate return on investment (ROI) through a pilot project. (Find out more about the IBM Garage Methodology: https://www.ibm.com/garage/ method/.)

In closing, the authors and contributors of this book hope you succeed in all your data and AI adventures. We hope this book helps you to take that first or next step on your journey.

We close this book with one more quote traditionally attributed to Confucius:

"The journey of 1000 miles begins with a single step."
Confucius: 551 BC – 479 BC

Appendix A: Different Types of Data Storage Paradigms

This appendix provides brief descriptions of and comparisons between data warehouses, OLAP, OLTP, databases, data lakes, data marts, Hadoop, and data lakehouses.

Data Warehouse

The data warehouse, or enterprise data warehouse (EDW), is a system that aggregates data from different sources, integrating it into a single, central, consistent data store to support data analysis, data mining, AI, and ML. A data warehouse system enables an organization to run powerful analytics on huge volumes (terabytes and petabytes) of historical data in ways that a standard database cannot.

Data warehousing systems have been a part of BI solutions for more than three decades, but they have evolved recently with the emergence of new data types and data-hosting methods. Traditionally, a data warehouse was hosted on-premises—often on a mainframe computer—and its functionality was focused on extracting data from other sources, cleansing and preparing the data, and loading and maintaining the data in a relational database. More recently, a data warehouse might be hosted on a dedicated appliance or in the cloud, and most data warehouses have added analytics capabilities and data visualization and presentation tools.

A data warehouse provides a foundation for the following:

- Better data quality: A data warehouse centralizes data from a variety of data sources, such as transactional systems, operational databases, and flat files. It then cleanses it, eliminates duplicates, and standardizes it to create a single source of the truth.

- Faster business insights: Data from disparate sources limits the ability of decision-makers to set business strategies with confidence. Data warehouses enable data integration, allowing business users to leverage all of a company's data into each business decision.

- Smarter decision-making: A data warehouse supports large-scale BI functions such as data mining (finding unseen patterns and relationships in data), AI, and ML—tools data professionals and business leaders can use to get hard evidence for making smarter decisions in virtually every area of the organization, from business processes to financial management and inventory management.

- Gaining and growing competitive advantage: All the above combine to help an organization by finding more data opportunities more quickly than is possible from disparate data stores.

Data Warehouses and Online Analytical Processing (OLAP)

In a data warehouse environment like the one shown in Figure A.1, relational databases can be optimized for OLAP to facilitate analysis, enable queries on large numbers of records, and summarize data in many ways. Data stored in the data warehouse can also come from multiple sources.

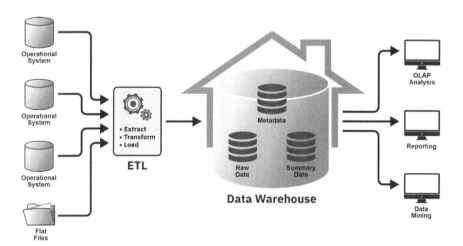

Figure A.1: Typical data warehouse architecture

Online Analytics Processing (OLAP) vs. Online Transactional Processing (OLTP)

The main distinction between the two systems is in their names: analytical vs. transactional. Each system is optimized for that type of processing.

OLAP is optimized to conduct complex data analysis for smarter decision-making. OLAP systems are designed for use by data scientists, business analysts, and knowledge workers, and they support BI, data mining, and other decision-support applications.

OLTP, on the other hand, is optimized to process a massive number of transactions. OLTP systems are designed for use by frontline workers (e.g., cashiers, bank tellers, hotel desk clerks) or for customer self-service applications (e.g., online banking, e-commerce, travel reservations). Other key differences between OLAP and OLTP include:

- Focus: OLAP systems enable users to extract data for complex analysis. To drive business decisions, the queries often involve large numbers of records. In contrast, OLTP systems are ideal for making simple updates, insertions, and deletions in databases. The queries typically involve just one or a few records.

- Data source: An OLAP database has a multidimensional schema, so it can support complex queries of multiple data facts from current and historical data. Different OLTP databases can be the source of aggregated data for OLAP, and they may be organized as a data warehouse. OLTP, on the other hand, uses a traditional DBMS to accommodate a large volume of real-time transactions.

- Processing time: In OLAP, response times are orders of magnitude slower than OLTP. Workloads are read-intensive, involving enormous data sets. For OLTP transactions and responses, every millisecond counts. Workloads involve simple read and write operations via Structured Query Language (SQL), requiring less time and less storage space.

- Availability: Because they don't modify current data, OLAP systems can be backed up less frequently. However, OLTP systems modify data frequently, since this is the nature of transactional processing. They require frequent or concurrent backups to help maintain data integrity.

Data Warehouse vs. Transactional Database

While this has been briefly touched on earlier, a database is built primarily for fast queries and transaction processing, not analytics. A database typically serves as the focused data store for a specific application, whereas a data warehouse stores data from any number (or even all) of the applications in an organization.

A database focuses on updating real-time data while a data warehouse typically has a broader scope, capturing current and historical data for predictive analytics, ML, and other advanced types of analysis.

Data warehouses are good foundations for a data system that uses AI and a data fabric architecture for several reasons:

1. Transactional databases are typically smaller and grow to only a few terabytes of data. The larger they grow, the larger the performance impact. Data warehouses are typically several hundred terabytes and can grow to petabytes.

2. There is a need to access and analyze data from many different sources to provide data scientists or business analysts the ability to make better decisions by leveraging different types of data.

3. Running analytical queries has a performance impact on any computer system and can take anywhere from multiple seconds to many minutes (and in some cases longer) to execute. While this is acceptable for reporting and BI, it is not acceptable for real-time transactions. Taking a banking transaction as an example, a user could be frustrated by waiting several minutes to withdraw cash or deposit a check. Because of the impact on performance by analytical queries on a transactional database, moving data to a warehouse becomes the norm and hence the need for these two systems.

Disadvantages of a Data Warehouse

The disadvantages of a data warehouse are centered around the multiple complexities that can result when data needs to be moved or replicated regularly, as data warehouses often require. These include costs, the fact that data is typically out of date or out of synch, and slower performance. Security issues can include the need to provide security to multiple environments and the problem that as additional users gain access to the data warehouse, that access creates security risks to personally identifiable, confidential, and sensitive data exposure risks.

Data Warehouse vs. Data Lake

A data warehouse gathers raw data from multiple sources into a central repository, structured using predefined schemas (for example, predefined tables each having a set of defined columns or fields) designed for data analytics. A data lake is a data warehouse without the predefined schemas. As a result, it enables more types of analytics than a data warehouse, as it enables the storage of data in many different formats as and when new data needs to be stored. Data lakes are commonly but not exclusively built on big data platforms such as Apache Hadoop.

Data Warehouse vs. Data Mart

A data mart is a subset of a data warehouse that contains data specific to a particular business line or department. Because they contain a smaller subset of data, data marts enable a department or business line to discover more-focused insights more quickly than possible when working with the broader data warehouse data set.

Data Warehouse Appliance

A data warehouse appliance is a preintegrated bundle of hardware and software—CPUs, storage, operating system, and data warehouse software—that a business can connect to its network and start using as is. A data warehouse appliance sits somewhere between cloud and on-premises implementations in terms of upfront cost, speed of deployment, ease of scalability, and management control.

Hadoop

Apache Hadoop is a collection of open-source software utilities that facilitates using a network of many computers to solve problems involving massive amounts of data and computation. The ecosystem is shown in Figure A.2. It provides a software framework for distributed storage and processing of large data sets using the MapReduce programming model.

Hadoop was originally designed for computer clusters built from commodity hardware, which is still the most common use. It has since also found use on clusters of higher-end hardware. All the modules in Hadoop are designed with a fundamental assumption that hardware failures are common occurrences and should be automatically handled by the framework.

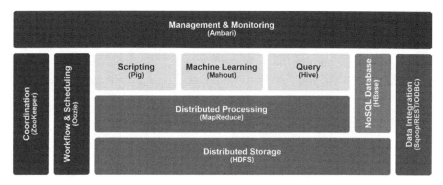

Figure A.2: Apache Hadoop ecosystem

The core of Apache Hadoop consists of a storage part, known as Hadoop Distributed File System (HDFS), and a processing part, which is a MapReduce programming model. Hadoop splits files into large blocks and distributes them across nodes in a cluster. It then transfers packaged code into nodes to process the data in parallel. This facilitates concurrent processing by splitting petabytes of data into smaller chunks and processing them in parallel on Hadoop commodity servers. Once processing is complete, Hadoop aggregates all the data from multiple servers to return a consolidated output back to the application.

This approach takes advantage of data locality, where nodes manipulate the data to which they have access. This enables the data set to be processed faster and more efficiently than it would be within a more-conventional supercomputer architecture that relies instead on a parallel file system where computation and data are distributed via high-speed networking. Hadoop is considered by many to be a form of data lake.

Data Lake vs. Data Lakehouse

A data lake, as shown in Figure A.3, is a centralized data repository for management of extremely large data volumes and serves as a foundation for collecting and analyzing structured, semi-structured, and unstructured data in its native format. This can help organization derive new insights, make better predictions, and achieve improved optimization. Unlike traditional data warehouses, data lakes can process video, audio, logs, texts, social media, and sensor, as well as data and documents to power apps, analytics, and AI.

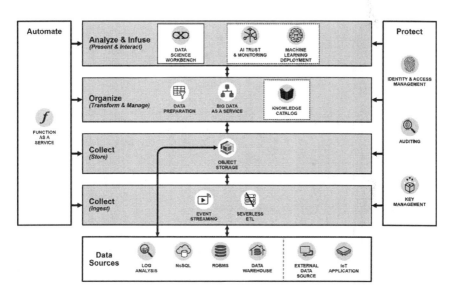

Figure A.3: Example data lake architecture

Data warehouses and data lakes each evolved to meet a set of specific technology and business needs and values. As organizations often need both, there has been increasing demand for convergence of both technologies. Thus, the data lakehouse was born. A data lakehouse couples the cost benefits of a data lake with the data structure and data management capabilities of a data warehouse. A more simplified way to think of a data lakehouse is as an evolution of the analytic data repository that supports acquisition to refinement, delivery, and storage with an open table format. Without going into detail, it is defined as part of Apache Iceberg (see https://iceberg.apache.org) and was designed for handling huge analytic data sets. It is used in production where a single table can contain tens of petabytes of data and the data can be read without a distributed SQL engine.

A data lakehouse is designed to help organizations get more from their existing investment in data warehouses and data lakes. It supports the existence of both through access to and management of a larger variety of combined data for increased flexibility.

Data lakehouse use can provide users with the following abilities:

- Understand and anticipate customer behaviors with more complete, governed insights.

- Spot patterns and trends to reduce waste and overhead through more diverse analytic and AI techniques.

- Promote auditability and transparency with metadata-powered, native data access in a governed data lake.

- Speed time to value with self-service data exploration and discovery for users.

- Increase collaboration and reduce the time and cost of managing disparate systems and tools in an integrated environment.

- Turn open-source and ecosystem investments into innovation opportunities with enterprise-ready, secure data lakes.

Data lakehouses have the ability to:

- Reuse the data lake for 360-degree customer and operational intelligence, governance, and risk and compliance reporting

- Ingest and integrate with transactional, operational, and analytical data to promote a complete insight

- Extend information architectures to provide the right data at the right time on a common foundation for staging, storage, and access

- Build and maintain a data foundation that powers data cataloging, curation, exploration, and discovery needs

- Take a hybrid approach to access any data from any locations spanning years of records to real-time data

- Integrate and expand analytics across multiple data repositories to drive innovation and optimization at scale

As organizations continue to move parts of their data estates and processing into hybrid multiclouds, data lakes and data lakehouses help provide optimum value, building on the following principles:

- Secure data-sharing across multiple teams accessing enterprise data: Organizations should be able to rely on data lake governance that houses raw structured and unstructured data—trusted, secured, and governed—with automated privacy and security anywhere.

- Presence of data-integration tools that combine data from disparate sources into valuable data sets: Tools such as ETL, controlled data replication, and data virtualization can extract large volumes of data from source systems and load it where applicable to a data warehouse.

- Via data virtualization, organizations should be able to query data directly in the data lake without duplication or movement.

Notices and Disclaimers

The content herein represents the personal views of the authors and not necessarily that of IBM or any other company they have worked for. Copyright © 2022 by International Business Machines Corporation (IBM). No part of this document may be reproduced or transmitted in any form without written permission from IBM.

Information in this publication (including information relating to products that have not yet been announced by IBM) has been reviewed for accuracy as of the date of initial publication and could include unintentional technical or typographical errors. IBM shall have no responsibility to update this information. This document is distributed "as is" without any warranty, either express or implied. In no event shall IBM be liable for any damage arising from the use of this information, including but not limited to, loss of data, business interruption, loss of profit, or loss of opportunity. IBM products and services are warranted according to the terms and conditions of the agreements under which they are provided.

IBM products are manufactured from new parts or new and used parts.

In some cases, a product may not be new and may have been previously installed. Regardless, warranty terms apply.

Any statements regarding IBM's future direction, intent, or product plans are subject to change or withdrawal without notice.

Performance data contained herein was generally obtained in controlled, isolated environments.

References in this document to IBM products, programs, or services does not imply that IBM intends to make such products, programs, or services available in all countries in which IBM operates or does business.

Workshops, sessions, and associated materials may have been prepared by independent session speakers and do not necessarily reflect the views of IBM. All materials and discussions are provided for informational purposes only, and are neither intended to nor shall constitute legal or other guidance or advice to any individual participant or their specific situation.

Information concerning non-IBM products was obtained from the suppliers of those products, their published announcements, or other publicly available sources. IBM has not tested those products in connection with this publication and cannot confirm the accuracy of performance, compatibility, or any other claims related to non-IBM products. Questions on the capabilities of non-IBM products should be addressed to the suppliers of those products. IBM does not warrant the quality of any third-party products or the ability of any such third-party products to interoperate with IBM's products. IBM expressly disclaims all warranties, expressed or implied, including but not limited to the implied warranties of merchantability and fitness for a particular purpose.

The provision of the information contained herein is not intended to, and does not, grant any right or license under any IBM patents, copyrights, trademarks, or other intellectual property right.

IBM, the IBM logo, ibm.com, IBM Watson, With Watson, and IBM Cloud Pak are trademarks of International Business Machines Corporation, registered in many jurisdictions worldwide. Other product and service names might be trademarks of IBM or other companies. A current list of IBM trademarks is available on the Web at "Copyright and Trademark Information" at https://www.ibm.com/legal/copytrade

Amazon Web Services, AWS are registered trademarks of Amazon Web Services, Inc, https://aws.amazon.com/trademark-guidelines/

Apache, Apache Spark, Hadoop, Spark are registered trademarks of the Apache Software foundation. www.apache.org/foundation/marks/

AWS is a registered trademarks of Amazon Web Services Inc. https://aws.amazon.com/trademark-guidelines/

Azure is a registered trademark of Microsoft Corporation. www.microsoft.com/en-us/legal/intellectualproperty/trademarks/en-us.aspx

Google is a registered trademark of Google LLC. www.google.com/permissions/trademark/trademark-list/

Kubernetes is a registered trademark of The Linux Foundation. https://www.linuxfoundation.org/trademark-list/

Python is a registered trademark of the Python Software Foundation. www.python.org/psf/trademarks/

Red Hat, OpenShift are registered trademark of Red Hat Inc. www.redhat.com/en/about/trademark-guidelines-and-policies

RStudio is a trademark of RStudio, Inc. https://www.rstudio.com/about/trademark/

The Jupyter Trademark is registered with the U.S. Patent and Trademark Office.